*Popular Organization
and Democracy
in Rio de Janeiro*

POPULAR ORGANIZATION and DEMOCRACY in RIO de JANEIRO

A Tale of Two Favelas

ROBERT GAY

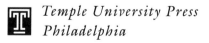 *Temple University Press*
Philadelphia

Temple University Press, Philadelphia 19122
Copyright © 1994 by Temple University
Published 1994
Printed in the United States of America

The paper used in this publication meets the minimum requirements of American
National Standard for Information Sciences—Permanence of Paper for Printed Library
Materials, ANSI Z39.48-1984 ⊚

Library of Congress Cataloging-in-Publication Data
Gay, Robert, 1958–
    Popular organization and democracy in Rio de Janeiro : a tale of two favelas /
Robert Gay.
        p.   cm.
    Includes bibliographical references and index.
    ISBN 1-56639-119-9 (alk. paper). — ISBN 1-56639-120-2 (pbk. : alk. paper)
    1. Slums—Political aspects—Brazil—Rio de Janeiro.   2. Squatter settlements—
Political aspects—Brazil—Rio de Janeiro.   3. Vila Brasil (Rio de Janeiro, Brazil)
4. Vidigal (Rio de Janeiro, Brazil)   5. Rio de Janeiro (Brazil)—Politics and government.
6. Neighborhood government—Brazil—Rio de Janeiro.   I. Title.
HV4075.R53G39   1994
307.3'36416'098153—dc20

                                                                        93-11105

For James, Valerie, Lindsey, and Devon

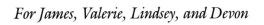

Contents

Photographs

Maps and Tables

MAPS

TABLES

Acknowledgments

This book is the product of many contributions by many people, from academic advisors and dissertation committee members to readers, editors, field contacts, colleagues, and friends. I am particularly indebted, however, to Peter Evans, Renato Boschi, Dietrich Rueschemeyer, John Stephens, Scott Mainwaring, Marc Forster, Jeff Lesser, Judith Chubb, Doris Braendel, Paulo Banana, John Klebin, Maurício Abreu, Paulo Cavallieri, Pedro Celso, Cleide Quitéria dos Santos, Ray Barley, Berta Treiger, Maria Alice, and all my friends at the Pastoral de Favelas. I can honestly say that without your help this project would not have come to fruition.

Of course, the real heroes of this book are my many friends in Vila Brasil and Vidigal. Their courage and determination in the face of public ignorance and discrimination are a constant source of inspiration. I would like to thank all of you for tolerating my presence, for putting up with my many questions, for helping me with my survey, and most important of all, for becoming my friends. Thank you once again Cleonice, Boarnerges, Carlinhos, Paulinho, Duque, Claudio, Anna Paula, Ivanite, Eliane, Erica, and Marileide. This was an experience that I will never forget.

Finally, I would like to thank my parents for uprooting me when I was thirteen years old to live in a strange land called Brazil, and to thank my wife and my daughter for all their patience, love, and understanding.

*Popular Organization
and Democracy
in Rio de Janeiro*

INTRODUCTION

Latin America's urban poor are often portrayed as the innocent victims of repressive and exclusionary regimes.[1] Victims they undoubtedly are; innocent, however, they are not. Indeed, there is increasing evidence from a variety of contexts that the urban poor have been active, organized, and aggressive participants in the political process and that popular organizations, in particular, have had a significant impact on the relationship between the urban poor and political elites.[2]

Two Favelas

This book tells the story of Vila Brasil and Vidigal, two *favelas*, or slum neighborhoods, in the city of Rio de Janeiro, Brazil.[3] It tells of their constant struggle for survival, of their unceasing efforts to organize, and of their longstanding and complex relationship with local politicians and administrators. To the outsider, the two favelas appear very much the same. Both are settled illegally on plots of privately owned land, both are inhabited by individuals and families that are unable to afford accommodation in the formal housing market, and both enjoy only limited and substandard access to a range of basic urban services. On closer inspection, however, the two favelas are significantly different.

Vila Brasil is one of many favelas in Rio that pursue their interests by exchanging votes for favors. This means that before every election the president of Vila Brasil's neighborhood association makes it known that the favela will vote en masse for the highest bidder among all candidates for public office. The president's strategy has proven to be highly successful over the course of the past ten years or so. In fact, it has been largely responsible for the transformation of Vila Brasil into one of the best-served favelas in the region.

The neighborhood association in Vidigal has also had its fair share of success. It is not, however, in the business of selling votes, and it steadfastly refuses to support candidates of the kind that are regularly entertained by the president of Vila Brasil. The leaders of the neighborhood association in Vidigal make it known that no one will be allowed to campaign in the area on the basis of what he or she has done for the favela in the past or promises to do in the future. This does not mean that public works and personal gifts to the community are not rewarded at the ballot box but that the neighborhood association refuses to encourage, facilitate, or endorse such forms of political behavior.

The difference between the two favelas' political strategies can be explained in terms of the different relationship that developed between the leadership of their respective neighborhood associations and the so-called popular movement that confronted the military in Rio de Janeiro in the late 1970s and early 1980s. To many, the mobilization of popular protest represented an interesting but largely inconsequential stage in the transition to democracy. To others, it heralded the dawn of a new political era. Whatever its larger implications, the mobilization of popular protest had a profound and lasting impact on the social and political life of the population of many of Rio's five hundred or so favelas.

The emergence of a popular movement in Rio meant that the residents of Vidigal were able to challenge and eventually overcome an attempt to remove the community from its present site in October 1977.

It also meant that what subsequently emerged as the leadership of the favela was exposed to a very different vision of the political process. In Vila Brasil, the emergence of a popular movement also led to important changes in the political organization of the favela, but in ways that both challenged *and* reinforced the relationship between the population of Vila Brasil and political elites.

This difference between the two favelas is important for two reasons. First, it determines both the nature and the broader consequences of each favela's participation in the political process. The success of the president of Vila Brasil in profiting from elections means that his many followers in the favela tend to support candidates who will buy their way into public office but who have little real concern for the plight of the urban poor. It also means that voters in Vila Brasil are less likely to support candidates who refuse to or are unable to buy votes. Promises of a better life or of a more just society ten or fifteen years down the road tend to fall on deaf ears in the favela. Voters in Vila Brasil are more concerned with the here and now, with the supply of electricity and water to the favela and with the concrete concerns of everyday favela life.

By way of contrast, the decision of the leadership of Vidigal to turn its back on patronage politics and to pursue its interests via alternative channels means that voters in the favela face very different political issues. The neighborhood association in Vidigal is no longer dependent on selling votes and, as a consequence, is no longer as susceptible to attempts at political blackmail. In Vidigal, therefore, the cycle of dependency has been broken. To do well as a politician in Vidigal, it is necessary to talk not only about the provision of electricity and water in the favela but also about the more general issues of wages, police violence, education, and health care.

This difference between the two favelas is also important, however, in that it reveals that popular political participation is as much the product of collective organization and resistance as it is of the actions and decisions of politicians and administrators. And, as such, this book is not solely, or even primarily, about two favelas in Rio de Janeiro but is also about the many different forms of popular organization, about the changing nature of the relationship between popular organizations and political elites, and about the role of popular organizations in the process of political change.

Popular Organization and Political Change

The 1985 inauguration of Tancredo Neves as Brazil's first civilian president in twenty-one years marked the end of a long and uncertain transition to democracy. The final stages of this transition witnessed the emergence of an increasingly organized and vocal popular movement. The popular movement consisted of a bewildering array of different elements, from labor unions and professional organizations to neighborhood associations and church groups. The popular movement was important in that it provided a measure of resistance to the regime, played a prominent role in the organization of a number of large-scale public protests, and formed the basis for a new political party, the Partido dos Trabalhadores (PT), in 1979.[4]

The emergence of a popular movement and the explosion of popular protest against the authoritarian regime led some to predict that the withdrawal of the military would be accompanied by a transformation in the nature of Brazilian politics and a shift in the balance of class power. The hope was that the popular movement would destroy the legitimacy of the authoritarian state; undermine popular support for elitist political parties; and sweep the radical, democratic Left to power.[5]

The return to democracy proved something of a disappointment, however. It was accompanied by widespread popular demobilization, by the eclipse of the political Left, by the continued success of politicians with close ties to the military regime, and by the resurgence of political leaders from Brazil's preauthoritarian past. It appeared, therefore, that the proliferation of popular organizations and the explosion of popular protest in the late 1970s and early 1980s had little impact on the nature of postauthoritarian politics.[6]

Elements of continuity between postauthoritarian, authoritarian, and even preauthoritarian Brazil have meant that accounts of the past two decades have largely ignored the role of popular organization and protest and focused instead on the decisions and actions of political elites.[7] This concern with the role of elites is by no means a product of the recent transition, however. Rather, it reflects the widely held belief that Brazil's participation in the world economy has given rise to a social-class structure that is characterized by a strong interventionist state and a weak and disorganized civil society.[8] Missing from this explanation, however, is an appreciation of the tension, or dynamic, inherent in the relationship *between* civil and political society in Brazil, a tension that reflects the way in which the popular classes were incorporated into the political process.

The exposure of what was essentially a primary product economy to the effects of capitalist competition in the core resulted in a delayed and somewhat restricted pattern of industrialization in Brazil and the emergence of a dispersed, heterogeneous, and largely unorganized working class.[9] As a consequence, working-class enfranchisement and political participation were initiated and, to a certain extent, constrained by elites competing for control of the state. The principal forms of popular political participation in contemporary Brazilian politics, clientelism and populism, continue to reflect this logic.[10]

Clientelism is a somewhat expansive concept that refers to particularistic and hierarchical exchange relationships between actors of different social status and wealth. As such, it encompasses both the relationship between lord and vassal in the countryside and the more contemporary and increasingly urban forms of face-to-face exchange between politician and voter.[11] Populism, on the other hand, refers to elite-led, multiclass mass movements of marginal or hitherto excluded groups in civil society. Like clientelism, however, populism is essentially a votes-for-patronage strategy based on the monopoly and selective distribution of public goods and the protection and expansion of political turf. Therefore, it too involves elements of political mobilization *and* control.[12]

Both clientelism and populism have been prominent and enduring features of the political landscape in Brazil.[13] More important, however, they have provided institutional mechanisms for interaction, exchange, and solidarity between elites and masses. The notion that civil society in Brazil is somehow weak, therefore, is essentially incorrect, the truth being that civil and political society are arranged, or articulated, in such a way as to make popular political organization on the basis of social class extremely difficult.[14]

Although enduring, such relationships are rarely stable, however, in the sense that patterns of interaction, exchange, and solidarity between elites and masses are subject to a never-ending process of challenge, adjustment, and renegotiation.[15] Therefore, it is the challenge, adjustment, and renegotiation of the relationship between civil and political society in Brazil that, perhaps more than anything else, holds the key to political change. And it is within this context that the events of the late 1970s and early 1980s that are dealt with in this book are of particular significance.[16]

Of course, the relationship between elites and masses and between civil and political society is an issue of central and longstanding interest to sociologists and social scientists in general, and certainly is not one that is idiosyncratic to the Brazilian case.[17] Furthermore, from Latin America to the postcommunist regimes of Eastern Europe and the former Soviet Union to the newly industrializing states of Southeast Asia, democracy has been embraced as a social, political, and economic panacea. It is already more than clear, however, that the establishment of basic political rights is a historic yet relatively small victory in the struggle for a more substantive form of social democracy that goes beyond participation at the ballot box. Thus, while this book is about the relationship between the urban poor and political elites in Rio de Janeiro, it is also a contribution toward the increasingly lively and compelling debate about political transitions, popular organization, and democracy in other parts of the globe.[18]

Popular Organization and the Favelas of Rio de Janeiro

Of the many different areas of Brazil that witnessed the emergence of a popular movement, Rio de Janeiro is perhaps the most interesting. Rio was the site of a number of large-scale public acts of protest against the military regime in the late 1970s and early 1980s. Rio also witnessed the

TABLE 1
Favela Population Growth in the Municipality of Rio de Janeiro, 1950–80

Year	Favela Population	Rate of Growth of Favela Population (%)	Population of Rio
1950	169,305	—	2,336,000
1960	335,063	97.9	3,307,167
1970	565,135	68.7	4,285,738
1980	722,424	27.8	5,180,413

SOURCE: Paulo F. Cavallieri, "Favelas Cariocas: Mudanças na Infra-estrutura," in Paulo F. Cavallieri, ed., *Quatro Estudos* (Rio de Janeiro: IPLANRIO, 1986), p. 20.

proliferation of popular organizations, primarily in the form of neighborhood associations. Finally, and most important, in Rio, perhaps more than elsewhere in Brazil, the popular movement extended its reach to the poorest, most severely disadvantaged elements of society, to the population of the city's innumerous and rapidly expanding favelas.

Popular visions of Rio inspire images of a steamy tropical paradise, of a busy cosmopolitan city surrounded by sun, sea, and vast stretches of golden sand. The reality of the place is rather different. A relatively small and physically compact area of the city corresponds to photographs that adorn travel brochures across the globe. Much of Rio and its hinterland, however, is violent, unserviced, and extremely poor. In fact, somewhere in the region of 14 percent of Rio's over six million inhabitants live in the five hundred or so favelas that dominate the city's urban landscape.[19]

Table 1 reveals that the population of Rio's favelas has been increasing steadily over the past few decades, both in absolute terms and as a percentage of the population of the city itself. Table 1 also shows that the rate of population growth in the favelas has slowed somewhat since the 1960s. This is, in part, because rates of immigration and population growth in the region have recently been on the decline. It is also, however, because a large number of favelas were physically removed in the 1960s and 1970s and because there is now little room for expansion in

TABLE 2

Favela Population of Rio de Janeiro by Region, 1980

Region	Favela Population	% of Total Regional Population	% of Total Municipal Favela Population
Central/South	205,977	14	28
North	417,527	19	58
West	98,920	7	14
Municipality	722,424	14	100

NOTE: In this table, the Central/South region consists of the administrative regions (RAs) of Copacabana, Botafogo, Lagoa, Centro, Tijuca, Vila Isabel, Santa Teresa, Rio Comprido, São Cristóvão, and Portuária. The North Region consists of the RAs of Engenho Novo, Méier, Ramos, Irajá, Madureira, Anchieta, Penha, Ilha do Governador, and Paquetá. The West region consists of the RAs of Jacarepaguá, Barra da Tijuca, Campo Grande, Santa Cruz, and Bangu.

SOURCE: Paulo F. Cavallieri, "Favelas Cariocas: Mudanças na Infra-estrutura," in Paulo F. Cavallieri, ed., *Quatro Estudos* (Rio de Janeiro: IPLANRIO, 1986), p. 20.

existing favelas. The saturation of space in the favelas of Rio has meant that the urban poor have been pushed increasingly toward the periphery as ever greater numbers are forced to pursue substandard housing options at ever greater distances from the city center.[20]

Table 2 shows how unevenly distributed throughout Rio de Janeiro the favela population is. By far the highest concentrations are to be found in the industrial and commercial districts to the north of the city center. (See Map 1.) In fact, in 1980, somewhere in the region of 19 percent of the population of northern Rio resided in favelas, a figure that exceeded 50 percent in some neighborhoods. A far smaller proportion of the city's favela population live in the southern and central parts of the city. This is not because the areas in and around the city center and wealthy residential districts are any less desirable but because in the past such areas have been consistent targets for the removal of favelas.

Table 2 also reveals that the western and most distant neighborhoods

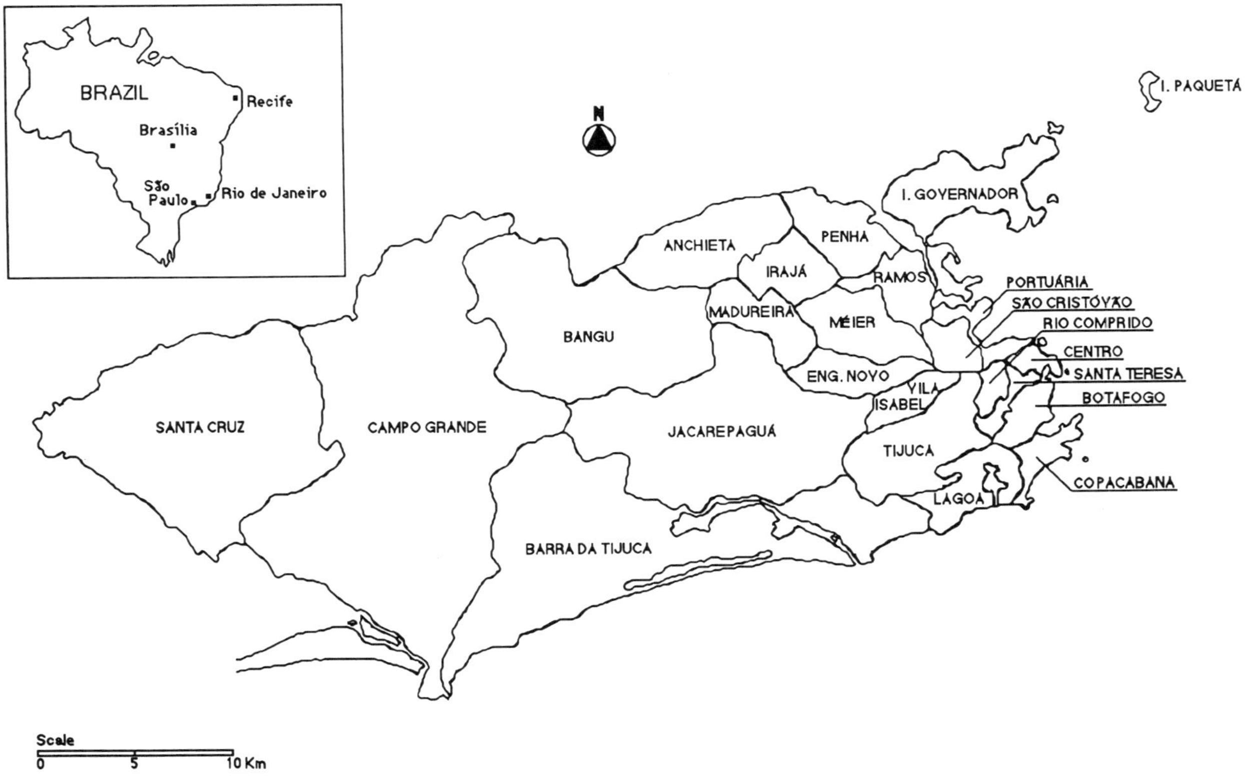

MAP 1. The Municipality of Rio de Janeiro with Inset of Brazil

I. PAQUETÁ

I. GOVERNADOR

PENHA

RAMOS

IRAJÁ

ANCHIETA

MADUREIRA

MÉIER

ENG. NOVO

VILA ISABEL

TIJUCA

JACAREPAGUÁ

BANGU

BARRA DA TIJUCA

CAMPO GRANDE

SANTA CRUZ

LAGOA

PORTUÁRIA
SÃO CRISTÓVÃO
RIO COMPRIDO
CENTRO
SANTA TERESA
BOTAFOGO
COPACABANA

N

BRAZIL

Recife

Brasília

Rio de Janeiro

São Paulo

Scale

10 Km
5
0

TABLE 3

Distribution of Favelas of Rio de Janeiro
by Size, 1980

Number of Inhabitants	Frequency	%	Population	%
<1000	224	60	82,073	12
1001–5000	113	30	248,436	34
>5000	39	10	391,915	54
Total	376	100	722,424	100

SOURCE: Paulo F. Cavallieri, "Favelas Cariocas: Mudanças na Infra-estrutura," in Paulo F. Cavallieri, ed., *Quatro Estudos* (Rio de Janeiro: IPLANRIO, 1986), p. 21.

of Rio house an even smaller percentage of the city's favela population. This region is rapidly becoming the poorest in the municipality, however. Many of those who were removed from favelas in the central districts of the city in the 1960s and 1970s were relocated to the vast and now dilapidated public-housing projects that litter the region, and in recent years the western districts more than any other part of Rio have witnessed the proliferation of new favelas and the establishment of illegal subdivisions.[21]

Table 3 shows that the majority of the favelas in Rio are small settlements of less than a thousand people and that, despite their number, they account for a relatively insignificant proportion of the city's favela population. The few really large favelas, on the other hand, account for the vast majority of the city's favela population. Most of these large favelas can be found in the northern parts of the city, often in close proximity to each other. The largest of these favela agglomerations, an area in Ramos known as Maré, houses an estimated 65,000 people.[22] The largest single favela in Rio is Rocinha. Located on prime real estate in the heart of one of the city's wealthiest residential districts, the population of Rocinha is estimated to be somewhere between the official estimate of 35,000 and the popular estimate of 200,000![23]

Finally, Table 4 reveals that while the settlement of new favelas in

TABLE 4
Distribution of Favelas of Rio de Janeiro by Year of Occupation, 1981

Year of Occupation	%
Before 1920	6
1921–1940	23
1941–1960	44
1961–1981	27
Total	100

SOURCE: Paulo F. Cavallieri, "Favelas Cariocas: Mudanças na Infra-estrutura," in Paulo F. Cavallieri, ed., *Quatro Estudos* (Rio de Janeiro: IPLANRIO, 1986), p. 22.

Rio has continued apace over a period of sixty years or so, the majority were built before 1960.[24] Most of the earliest favelas were established in the southern part of the city. Since then, however, the locus of favela settlement has shifted to the northern and, more recently, the western districts of Rio. This pattern of settlement reflects both the impact of eradication programs in the 1960s and 1970s and the saturation of space for the establishment of new favelas on land close to the city center.

Like similar settlements in other parts of the globe, the favelas of Rio were, and still are, built on vacant plots of private or government-owned land.[25] As such, they have been under almost constant threat of removal and have been denied all but the most basic urban services. Over time, however, all but a few favelas have undergone a process of urbanization, either through government intervention or as a result of the organization of self-help projects. Either way, the quality of services in even the most urbanized of Rio's favelas falls far short of standards required of "regular" neighborhoods in surrounding areas.[26] A survey of 364 favelas in Rio in 1981, for example, found that while the majority enjoyed some form of piped water provision, only 6 percent drew their water from an officially installed system. The survey also found that 32 percent of the favelas that were surveyed relied almost exclusively on water drawn from springs, wells, or water outlets.[27]

The collection of sewage in Rio's favelas is even more precarious. Only 14 percent of the 364 favelas surveyed in 1981 reported that their communities were served by a fairly extensive sewage system, and only 1 percent reported that they enjoyed access to an officially installed system. Fully 62 percent, on the other hand, said that there was no sewage collection to speak of in the favela, and in 48 percent raw sewage flowed through the streets in open ditches.[28] In all but a few cases, sewage ditches also served as drainage channels for rainwater. This means that during the rainy season the sewage ditches commonly flood their banks into adjacent houses. The combination of inadequate drainage, the accumulation of garbage, and the precarious construction of the majority of the buildings in Rio's favelas also means that the rainy season is accompanied by the very real threat of major and often fatal landslides.

The favelas of Rio are also at a severe disadvantage in terms of a range of other basic urban services. They seldom enjoy more than limited access to the most basic educational and medical facilities, are located far from major commercial centers, and are more often than not badly served by transportation networks. The majority of the favelas are also unpoliced, and it is largely because they have been abandoned by the state that they have increasingly fallen prey to elements involved in the drug trade. All but a few favelas in the city of Rio provide cover for armed gangs that peddle cocaine and marijuana to local elites, to tourists, and, increasingly, to the inhabitants of the favelas themselves. These gangs are often the perpetrators of extreme violence in their dealings with local police, who are themselves often involved in the buying and selling of drugs, and in their dealings with rival gangs. They are also, however, a source of welfare in their own favelas, playing the occasional role of Robin Hood in return for public support and the protection of anonymity.[29]

As one might expect, the population of Rio's favelas consists primarily of the poorer working-class elements of *carioca* (Rio) society, although in recent years there has been a slow but noticeable influx of middle-class families into such areas.[30] Although data are scarce, surveys of individual favelas in Rio have found that the vast majority of the population is gainfully employed (women less so than men) in a wide variety of different unskilled or semiskilled occupations associated primarily with the city's service economy. These same surveys have also found considerable variation in household income in the favelas, with a median that is somewhere in the region of one-and-a-half to five minimum salaries.[31]

Not surprisingly, the population of Rio's favelas is also among the least educated elements of carioca society. Surveys have revealed that the majority of the present-day adult population of the favelas left school well before completing primary school and that only a small percentage completed secondary school or enrolled in higher education. The educational profile of the favelas is changing somewhat with the influx of middle-class elements into such areas and with the tendency for younger members of the population to stay in school longer. It is still the case, however, that the majority of young adults leave before completing their high school education.[32]

The many disadvantages faced by the favelas and the harsh and often tragic nature of favela life have taught the population of such areas to fend for itself. Over the years, therefore, the population of the favelas has devised any number of strategies for ensuring its survival, from attaching itself to political elites to organizing popular protest. At the center of these efforts has been the neighborhood association. All but a few of the favelas in existence in Rio today boast a neighborhood association. As we shall see, however, these organizations have played very different roles at different junctures in the region's long and checkered political history.[33]

1

THE POLITICS OF
URBAN SURVIVAL

No visitor to Rio can fail to be impressed by the contrast between the city's stunning physical beauty and the squalor of much of its urban environment, so much so that a visit to one of the region's favelas has become an essential stop on many a tour. It is as if the city has finally come to terms with the fact that the favelas are a permanent and essential feature of everyday life. If such an accommodation exists, however, it is both fragile and of recent origin. For until the mid 1970s, the favelas had been widely regarded as a form of cancer to be cut out and removed.

All attempts to rid Rio of its favelas have ended in failure, however. They have failed for many of the same reasons that similar policies have failed elsewhere in Latin America: rapid rates of population growth and rural-to-urban migration, rising levels of urban unemployment and underemployment, reliance by a significant element of the local political elite on the population of the favelas as a cheap source of votes, and, finally, the increasing adeptness of the residents of Rio's favelas themselves to articulate and defend their own interests.

The evolution of what is a longstanding and complex relationship between the population of Rio's favelas and political elites can be divided into four relatively distinct periods: the initial emergence and consolidation of the favelas (1850–1945), attempts by local elites to enlist the population of the favelas' political support (1945–62), efforts to physically remove all favelas from the city (1962–74), and finally, the attempt by local elites to rearticulate the relationship between the population of the favelas and the newly democratic state (1974–86).

Urbanization, Urban Poverty, and the Favelas: 1850–1945

The second half of the nineteenth century witnessed the transformation of the city of Rio de Janeiro from a sleepy colonial entrepôt to the undisputed commercial, financial, administrative, and cultural center of Brazil's Old Republic. This transformation was accompanied, however, by a dramatic increase in the size of Rio's urban working class and the emergence of a severe housing crisis.[1]

The presence of an increasingly large and unruly working class and the unsanitary nature of much of Rio's low-income housing moved local governing elites to consider ways of removing and relocating the urban poor. One way was to persuade industrialists to provide housing for their workers. This option was pursued by the state in the late 1880s and resulted in the construction of a token number of *vilas operárias* by local textile manufacturers, bankers, and construction firms.[2] Another way was the physical removal of working-class housing from downtown Rio and the forced relocation of the urban poor to the suburbs. This option was pursued by the state in 1904 when it embarked on a massive program of urban redevelopment.[3] Urban redevelopment did little to resolve the issue of housing for the urban poor, however. It simply meant that the occupants of working-class hostels and boarding houses in downtown Rio found similar accommodation elsewhere in the city or that they staked their claim to a plot of land in the favelas that subsequently emerged on Rio's hillsides.[4]

Over the next thirty years or so, both the number and the population of Rio's favelas increased steadily as dislocations associated with World War I, the Great Depression, the eclipse of the local coffee economy, and substantial rates of internal and international migration combined to swell the ranks of the country's then capital city.[5] Then in 1937, the state passed legislation prohibiting the construction of new dwellings and the physical improvement of existing dwellings in the favelas.[6] It was not until 1937, therefore, that the state officially recognized that the favelas were more than a temporary solution to problems associated with rapid rates of urbanization.[7]

The attempt by the state to restrict the expansion of existing favelas in Rio was accompanied in the early 1940s by wholesale favela removal and by further attempts to provide subsidized low-income housing. The outcome was the construction in 1942 of three highly publicized public-housing projects known as Parques Proletários. The Parques Proletários were more than public-housing projects, however, in that they were designed not only to accommodate but also to isolate and control the urban poor. For example, each resident was issued an identification card that was to be presented on entry to the parks' gates, which were then closed for the night at ten o'clock. At nine o'clock the administrator of each park would use a loudspeaker system to lecture his wards on issues of public morality![8]

The Parques Proletários were not a great success, in the sense that the population that was removed from the city's favelas far exceeded the small number of housing units that were made available. The Parques Proletários were important, however, in that they were indicative of the way that local elites understood and hoped to address the problem of urban poverty in Rio.

The Beginnings of Popular Political Participation: 1945–62

The overthrow of Getúlio Vargas and the establishment of popular democracy in Brazil in 1945 meant something of a change in the relationship between the state and the population of the favelas in Rio in that it brought an end to the more authoritarian solutions to the problem of urban poverty. Instead of simply removing the favelas, the state and the Catholic church in Rio now sought to encourage the physical consolidation and political organization of favela neighborhoods in situ.[9] This change in state policy and the involvement of the Catholic church owed less to a newfound commitment to the principles of democracy, however, than to a generalized fear of the massed ranks of the urban working class. Essentially, therefore, the consolidation and organization of the favelas in Rio were pursued as a means of political control.[10]

Of particular concern was the possibility that an increasingly large and marginal favela population would provide a rich source of votes for the Partido Comunista (PC). The PC fared surprisingly well in municipal elections in Rio in 1947, and it was largely the specter of a communist-inspired urban revolt, made all the more real by the postwar freeze between the United States and the Soviet Union, that prompted the creation of church and state agencies with a mandate to intervene in the favelas.[11] The most important of these institutions were the Fundação Leão XIII, created in 1947; the Cruzada São Sebastião, created in 1955; and the Serviço Especial de Recuperação de Favelas e Habitações Anti-Higiênicas (SERFHA), created one year later.[12]

All three institutions contributed to the physical consolidation of the favelas in that they were responsible for designing, financing, and implementing a wide variety of small public works projects. All three institutions were also involved in the organization and political orientation of neighborhood associations in the favelas. Ultimately, however, the activities of the Fundação Leão XIII, the Cruzada São Sebastião, and SERFHA were compromised to serve the interests of specific and often competing political elites.

Of particular significance in this regard was the emergence of Carlos Lacerda as a prominent member of the anti-Vargas coalition in Rio during the late 1940s and early 1950s. In 1948 Lacerda launched an attack on federal government policy toward the favelas in Rio, arguing that problems associated with urban poverty could no longer be resolved by purely repressive means. In this sense, Lacerda's understanding of the problem of the favelas mirrored that which led to the creation of the Fundação Leão XIII, the Cruzada São Sebastião, and SERFHA. In 1960, however, Lacerda was elected governor of the recently created state of Guanabara following the transfer of the nation's capital to Brasília. Within two years of taking office, Lacerda effectively silenced the

Cruzada São Sebastião, assumed control of the Fundação Leao XIII, and abolished SERFHA.[13]

It was not that Lacerda opposed state intervention in the favelas— far from it. It was a question of who reaped the benefits of this process. In the case of the Fundação Leão XIII and the Cruzada São Sebastião, Lacerda's intent was to bring an end to the activities of institutions that were not under his personal political control. In the case of SERFHA, Lacerda was under considerable pressure from members of the local political elite, who claimed that the agency was interfering with their role as intermediaries between the population of the favelas and the state.[14]

In an era when little could be done without the personal intervention of a member of the political elite, elected officials, public administrators, and candidates for public office in Rio exploited the lack of basic urban services in the favelas and the ever-present threat of removal as a cheap source of votes. They did this by patronizing local sports and social clubs, by sponsoring small public works projects, and by greasing the palm of local favela leaders. These leaders, otherwise known as *cabos eleitorais*, then worked as intermediaries between political elites and the population of the favelas at large and were responsible for turning out the vote on election day.[15]

The residents of Rio's favelas, for their part, had little choice but to participate in this process by courting the favor of politicians and public administrators. Over time, however, many leaders of favelas in Rio learned to take advantage of what was clearly an unequal and exploitative relationship by demanding more for their votes and by holding out for the highest bidder. More important was the fact that by the early 1960s a small but nonetheless significant number of neighborhood associations in Rio were refusing to accept any form of mediation between the population of the favelas and the state. SERFHA, under the tutelage of José Artur Rios, was partly responsible for this in that it had been promoting the organization of neighborhood associations in Rio that were independent of both political elites and state institutions. And it was this, more than anything, that led to SERFHA's demise at the hands of Carlos Lacerda in 1962.

Authoritarian Solutions: 1962–74

In 1962, the relationship between the population of the favelas and political elites in Rio took a decided turn for the worse in that demands for the revitalization of local capital and real estate markets were met by wholesale favela removal. The outcome was that between 1962 and 1974, an estimated 139,218 residents from eighty different favelas in Rio were forced to abandon their homes for publicly financed housing projects on the outskirts of the city.[16]

The removal of the favelas was facilitated, at the national level, by the intervention of the military in 1964 and by the end of any attempt, symbolic or otherwise, to include nonelite groups in the decision-making process. At the local level, it was facilitated by a series of administrative maneuvers that closed off avenues of potential conflict between the population of the favelas and the state and that reduced to a purely technical and administrative level the problem of relocating large numbers of the urban poor.[17] This meant that agencies that had been promoting the consolidation of the favelas were abruptly discontinued or redeployed while others were created to make way for wholesale favela removal.

Of particular importance in this regard were the abolition of SERFHA, the subordination of the Fundação Leão XIII to the authority of the local state, and the devolution of public responsibility for the favelas to the recently created administrative regions (RAs). Of more importance, however, was the creation in 1962 of the Cooperativa de Habitação Popular do Estado da Guanabara (COHAB). COHAB's mandate called for the removal *and* urbanization of selected favelas in Rio and for the construction of a large number of low-income housing units for the urban poor. As it turned out, however, COHAB was almost solely responsible for the first wave of favela removals, such that between 1962 and 1965 it accounted for the relocation of 42,000 residents from twenty-seven different favelas in Rio to public-housing projects in the suburbs.[18]

The association between authoritarian politics and authoritarian solutions was never absolute, however, as state policy toward the urban poor in Rio continued to reflect the interests of competing political elites. Thus, in 1968 a new agency, the Companhia de Desenvolvimento de Comunidade (CODESCO), for state intervention in the favelas was created with considerable financial backing from the United States Agency for International Development (USAID).[19] CODESCO was controlled by Lacerda's successor as governor of the state of Guanabara, Francisco Negrão de Lima (1965–71), who, as a member of the political opposition to the military, favored the consolidation of the favelas.[20]

In 1968 CODESCO sponsored the urbanization of three favelas in Rio de Janeiro, involving the regularization of land rights and the installation of lighting, water, and sewage systems.[21] CODESCO's success was short-lived, however, since four months after its creation the military government established yet another agency to intervene in the favelas, the Coordenadoria da Habitação de Interesse Social da Área Metropolitana do Rio de Janeiro (CHISAM). CHISAM was created with the expressed intention of resolving the tension between COHAB and CODESCO in Rio and of reestablishing the eradication of the favelas as the number-one policy priority. The outcome was that between 1968 and 1973, CHISAM was responsible for the removal of a further 90,000 residents from fifty different favelas, primarily from the wealthier districts of the city.

Few dared protest state policy toward the favelas, and popular resistance to the removal process was quickly and often brutally repressed. In March 1963, however, a group of favela leaders from the northern districts of the city joined forces to form the Federação de Associações de Favelas do Estado da Guanabara (FAFEG), which by 1968 claimed to represent 72 of the 132 neighborhood associations then in existence. The creation of a federation of favelas in Rio was important in that it led to the organization of two statewide favela neighborhood association congresses in 1964 and 1968 and in that it facilitated the mobilization of popular protest against the removal process. Ultimately, however, FAFEG's ability to resist the removal process was severely restricted by state government decrees in 1967 and 1969 that ruled that only one officially recognized neighborhood association was to be allowed in each favela or housing project.[22] These decrees gave the state ample opportunity to intervene in the affairs of recalcitrant favela organizations, so by the end of the 1960s FAFEG had been effectively shorn of its power to defend its members' interests. The federation was reactivated briefly in 1972 but, as before, remained under the relatively close control of the state.[23]

By 1974, however, the systematic removal of favelas had been abandoned as a policy failure. Removal was clearly not the answer as both the number of favelas and the size of Rio's favela population continued to increase unabated.[24] Furthermore, the public-housing projects to which many of the evicted had been relocated proved, once again, to be inadequate for the task. Expensive, badly constructed, and located miles from sources of employment, these new projects were soon abandoned by those who could not meet their monthly payments, who left them for favelas that had, until then at least, escaped the removal process.[25]

The year 1974 was also significant in that it marked the beginning of what was to become a decade-long transition to democracy. This transition meant increasing levels of political competition, which in turn meant an attempt by local political elites to reestablish their control over the population of Rio's favelas.[26]

Toward Democracy: 1974–86

THE ASCENDANCY OF ANTÔNIO DE PÁDUA CHAGAS FREITAS

From the late 1960s to the early 1980s, party politics in Rio was dominated by the figure of Antônio de Pádua Chagas Freitas. A carioca by birth, Chagas Freitas entered politics at an early age via a career in law and journalism. In 1954 he was elected to the Federal House of Representatives for the Partido Social Progressista (PSP), a feat he was to repeat in 1958 and again in 1962. At the time the PSP was a relatively small, regionally based party, with little support outside of Rio and São Paulo.[27]

Then, in 1965, the newly installed military regime curtailed the level of political competition in Brazil by purging the opposition of its more radical elements and by creating a biparty system consisting of the military-backed Aliança Renovadora Nacional (ARENA) and the Movimento Democrático Brasileiro (MDB). In Rio the military's purge cost the region many of its more progressive and combative politicians. Chagas Freitas took advantage of this exodus to wrest control of the MDB following its creation in 1965.

From 1969 on, politicians associated with the leadership of Chagas Freitas—otherwise known as *Chaguistas*—dominated the executive of the MDB in Rio. This enabled them to keep other factions within the party out of positions of power and to increase their share of the party's growing number of seats in Rio's State Assembly and in the Federal House of Representatives in the elections of 1970, 1974, and 1978.[28] Chagas Freitas's position as the undisputed leader of the MDB also led to his indirect election as governor of the state of Guanabara in 1970 and of the recently created state of Rio de Janeiro in 1978.[29]

The Chaguistas shared no common agenda or ideology. Theirs was an extremely pragmatic and conservative style of politics concerned almost exclusively with the consolidation of their political power in the region. Thus, while Rio de Janeiro was for a long time the only part of the country controlled by the opposition, the MDB's image in Rio was very much at odds with that of the national party. In fact, Chagas Freitas maintained a very good relationship with the military and was never perceived as a threat or as a source of opposition to the regime.

The cohesion of the Chaguistas was based on their personal and collective loyalty to Chagas Freitas. Chagas Freitas rewarded this loyalty by granting his followers privileged access to a wide range of public resources that were controlled by the local state. The Chaguistas then used this access to the state to cultivate their own political clienteles in the region through the selective distribution of public goods, services, political appointments, and jobs.[30]

The Chaguistas used their monopoly of state resources to construct political clienteles in all sectors of carioca society. Once again, however, the lack of basic urban services and the specter of removal meant that the Chaguistas' strategy enjoyed particular success among the population of Rio's favelas, a constituency that was to provide the Chaguistas and the MDB with the necessary ammunition for successive political victories throughout the 1970s.

THE MDB AND THE FAVELAS

In the years following the period of wholesale favela removal, little or no attention was paid to the "problem" of the favelas in Rio. This meant that while individual favelas were still singled out for removal, there was no attempt to resolve the issue of urban poverty. Then, in 1979, the MDB introduced a program of favela urbanization. The MDB's decision was motivated by four factors. The first was political liberalization, which meant that the more authoritarian solutions to urban poverty were, once again, out of favor and that wholesale favela removal was, therefore, no longer an option. The second factor was the offer of financial assistance from international aid agencies that were pressuring the Brazilian government to do something about the favelas. The third was the presence of an increasingly organized and militant favela movement that, since the reorganization of FAFERJ in 1979, had become increasingly intolerant of state policy toward the urban poor.[31] And finally, there were the 1982 elections to consider. The elections were the first for governor in Rio since 1965 and the first since the dismantling of the bi-party system in 1979. There was, therefore, a close association between the state's decision to urbanize the favelas and the MDB's aspirations for the forthcoming dispute.[32]

The state government's urbanization program was placed under the command of the municipal government of the city of Rio de Janeiro. The municipal government subsequently created a special agency, the Secretaria Municipal de Desenvolvimento Social (SMDS), to coordinate the project. Since the executive of the municipal government (the mayor of Rio de Janeiro) was at that time a nominee of the state governor, however, the SMDS enjoyed only a limited degree of political autonomy.

The SMDS was, nonetheless, something of a departure. It was, after all, the first government agency that had been created to deal specifically with the problem of the favelas. It was also, therefore, the first government agency to accept that urbanization was the state's responsibility, remembering that most government agencies of the time refused to set foot in the favelas since the favelas had no legal basis of existence. Finally, it was also the first time that any government had talked about urbanization, legalization of tenure, and popular participation in the planning process, all longstanding demands of the favela movement.

The SMDS, however, enjoyed only a limited degree of success, the principal reasons for its failure being a lack of financial resources and the opposition it encountered from politicians associated with governor Chagas Freitas. The SMDS's philosophy had been to create direct lines of communication between local government and the population of Rio's favelas. The SMDS was, therefore, threatening to undermine the role of local politicians as intermediaries.[33] The SMDS even went so far as attempting to bypass neighborhood associations, in recognition of the fact that the leaders of many favelas in Rio had closer ties with local political elites than with their own constituents. Thus, not only was the SMDS threatening to undermine the role of the clientelist politician, it was also threatening to interfere with the institutional structure by which the relationship between politician and voter was maintained.

The situation was made to look considerably worse in light of the elections in 1982. By all accounts the SMDS was the only state agency in Rio that was not fully geared toward the mobilization of support for the MDB's candidate for governor, Miro Teixeira. The hostility that this provoked from the party's rank and file resulted in the dismissal of Israel Klabin, the mayor of Rio, in May 1980. Four months later, Klabin's dismissal was followed by the resignation of the entire SMDS directorate.[34]

Júlio Coutinho, the mayor nominated to replace Klabin, could not, and did not, abandon a program that was already in full swing. He did, however, severely compromise the autonomy of the SMDS to accommodate the political demands of those who were strongly opposed to the program. This meant that the SMDS no longer interfered with the role of Chaguista politicians as intermediaries between the population of the favelas and the state and that, as a consequence, the program to urbanize the favelas was manipulated to serve the usual political ends. In other words, the SMDS became less concerned with urbanizing the favelas than with attending to the demands of leaders of favelas that were known supporters of the MDB.[35]

The SMDS's one success was the program to install public lighting in the favelas. The program was originally a joint project drawn up by the SMDS and LIGHT, the federal electricity company. It was LIGHT, however, that assumed responsibility for the program. By all accounts, the program was extremely well managed and relatively free from political interference, despite the fact that it threatened to do away with the *comissões de luz* that were an essential component of Chaguista power in the favelas.[36] When it was done, the program resulted in the provision of public lighting to nearly three hundred different favela communities, making it the first large-scale program of its kind in Rio. It is still something of an irony that the program was completed by the Partido Democrático Social (PDS), the party most closely associated with the military regime.[37]

THE RESURRECTION OF THE FAVELA MOVEMENT

The distribution of patronage by politicians associated with Chagas Freitas was only one element, albeit an important one, of the relationship between the MDB and the population of Rio's favelas. Others were the ever-watchful presence of the Fundação Leão XIII, which since the fusion of the states of Guanabara and Rio de Janeiro had assumed much of the responsibility for state intervention in the favelas, and the proximity between politicians within the MDB and the leadership of FAFERJ. In fact, it was the presence of the Fundação Leão XIII in the favelas and the subordination of FAFERJ to the interests of the local state that prompted the organization of a parallel, dissident federation of favelas in 1979.

The leadership of this parallel federation of favelas was highly critical of FAFERJ's failure to take issue with state policy toward the urban poor and of its open flirtation with Chaguista elements within the MDB. The leadership of the parallel federation argued that the federation should spend less time pandering to the interests of local politicians in return for small favors than aggressively pursuing the movement's more important demands such as the legalization of tenure, urbanization, and the return to democracy. It also felt that FAFERJ would only be in a position to do this if it changed the nature of its relationship with the state.[38] Emphasizing grass-roots mobilization and popular protest over the more clientelistic forms of interest representation, the leadership of the dissident federation proceeded to build a substantial following in the favelas of the region, especially among those communities with no prior history of political organization.[39]

The emergence of a parallel, more combative federation of favelas in Rio went hand in hand with a transformation in the nature of the relationship between the Catholic church and the urban poor. This transformation can be attributed, in part, to the impact of the Conference of Medellín in 1968 and the subsequent spread of liberation theology in Brazil. In Rio, however, it was also the direct result of the church's involvement with the attempt to challenge the removal of the favela of Vidigal in 1977. This experience moved the Archdiocese of Rio to champion the cause of the urban poor by creating the Pastoral de Favelas, an organization that was to provide invaluable juridical and organizational assistance to favelas despite determined resistance from the upper echelons of the church hierarchy.[40]

The reorganization of FAFERJ and the creation of the Pastoral de Favelas were important in that they played a prominent role in the rearticulation and mobilization of a favela movement in Rio in the late 1970s and early 1980s, a movement that, incidentally, was the first to question the logic of clientelist politics and, therefore, the apparent invincibility of the Chaguista regime.

THE 1982 ELECTIONS AND THE ASCENDANCY OF THE PDT

The elections for state governor in November 1982 marked the first time since 1965 that executive power was in the position to change hands in Brazil. As such, the elections presented the military and its accomplices with their first real political challenge. The military met this challenge by, once again, making wholesale changes to the rules of the political game.

The emergence of the MDB as a legitimate vehicle of popular protest in the mid 1970s was the principal motivation behind a series of electoral reforms introduced by the military in 1979. In abolishing a system that it had itself created in 1965, the military hoped to divide what was at best a fragile and heterogeneous political opposition. Two major parties emerged from the ranks of the MDB: the Partido do Movimento Democrático Brasileiro (PMDB)[41] and the Partido Popular (PP). The PP was the more conservative of the two, a distinction that was reflected in the partition of the former MDB in Rio. Chagas Freitas took the state and municipal administrations and those politicians closely associated with his leadership over to the PP, while the PMDB attracted the majority of the more progressive members of the former opposition party.

The military hoped to drive the opposition farther apart by prohibiting the formation of political alliances between parties in the elections in 1982. The national leadership of the PP and PMDB responded to this maneuver by bringing the two parties back together under the banner of the PMDB. There was considerable opposition to this move from within the rank and file of the PMDB in Rio because it meant the return to the fold of the Chaguistas. The reintegration of the PP and PMDB in Rio also had important ramifications for the favela movement.

The organization of a parallel federation of favelas in 1979 had mirrored divisions within the old MDB. The official FAFERJ organization enjoyed a close, some would say indecent, relationship with politicians close to Chagas Freitas and was subsequently supported by the PP. The parallel federation, on the other hand, was associated with the more progressive elements within the MDB and was supported by what became the PMDB. The merger of the PP and PMDB in Rio, therefore, led to a reconciliation of the two favela federations and to an agreement to support the PMDB's candidate for governor in 1982.

Elections for a new president and directorate of FAFERJ in April 1982 reflected the reconciliation of the two federations in that it witnessed the leader of what had been the parallel federation running for the office of president with the former president of the official FAFERJ as his vice-president. This pairing defeated a second group of favela leaders that wanted FAFERJ to take a more independent line from political parties in Rio and that was supported by, among others, the Partido dos Trabalhadores (PT). The PMDB provided considerable financial backing for both the incumbents' campaign and for the election itself and was represented, on the day, by a number of Chaguista politicians. The PMDB's influence on the election process was demonstrated further by the fact that the party's candidate for governor, Teixeira, was allowed to make a speech, whereas the PT's candidate, Lisâneas Maciel, was not.[42]

The two other parties of note in the elections for governor in 1982 were the PDS and the Partido Democrático Trabalhista (PDT). The PDS was a thin disguise for what was formerly ARENA, the party of the military regime until 1979. The PDT, on the other hand, was an entirely new political party formed by a group of exiled socialist intellectuals, political activists, and ex-politicians in Portugal in 1979.

The leader of the PDT was Leonel Brizola. Brizola had been governor of the state of Rio Grande do Sul when the military overthrew President

João Goulart in 1964. And, as one of the more radical elements within the precoup Partido Trabalhista Brasileiro (PTB), it was Brizola who had offered the most resistance to the military before fleeing into exile in neighboring Uruguay. From Uruguay, Brizola moved to Paris, to New York, and eventually to Portugal, where he began laying the ground work for a new PTB that was to be formed on his return to Brazil. It was Brizola's idea to create a nationalist, multiclass, and progressive political party that combined elements of *trabalhismo* (laborism) associated with the precoup PTB and European social democracy. What eventually became the PDT was to be a party that was committed to the redistribution of resources in favor of the poorest, most unorganized sectors of Brazilian society.[43]

In 1982, the PDT consisted of an uneasy combination of adherents to trabalhismo and elements of the socialist Left. It included politicians from the pre-1964 PTB, ex-ministers from the Goulart administration, and politicians that had recently fled the ranks of the PMDB. The majority of its candidates for office in 1982 were political unknowns, however. Despite this disadvantage, and the fact that the PDT had no tradition as a political party, Brizola was elected governor of Rio de Janeiro in what was perhaps the year's biggest surprise. That the PDT defeated the PDS in Rio was no great surprise in a state with a long tradition of opposition government (although the margin of votes between the PDT and the PDS was not, in fact, that great). More surprising, however, was the defeat of the PMDB, a party whose political control of the region had appeared, until 1982, to be extremely secure.[44]

One of the stipulations of the recently enacted electoral reforms was that ballots for each level of the election—governor, senator, federal deputy, state deputy, and city councilman—had to be cast for a single political party. Thus, if a voter opted for the PDS candidate for governor, he or she was obliged to vote for PDS candidates for senator, federal deputy, and so forth. Failure to do so meant that the ballot was annulled. The logic behind this stipulation (known as the *voto vinculado*) was that the strongest candidates for governor in each state would in all likelihood carry the rest of the votes at other levels of the dispute. In most states, the voto vinculado worked to the advantage of the PDS. In Rio de Janeiro, however, the strategy backfired. For not only was Brizola successful in winning the election for governor, he was also successful in electing a large number of PDT candidates to the Municipal Chamber, State Assembly, and Federal House of Representatives.

Brizola's victory, therefore, dealt a series of devastating blows to the PMDB in that it cost the party its control of state and municipal government and fairly decimated the ranks of those politicians most closely associated with Chagas Freitas. More important, however, it suggested that the reign of the Chaguistas in Rio had come to an abrupt end and that, given the choice, the voting population of Rio was no longer interested in tactics that had proven so effective in the past.[45]

The emergence of the PDT as a major political force in Rio was also significant in that, throughout the election campaign, the party made a clear commitment to the population of the region's favelas. The PDT's commitment generated substantial support for Brizola in 1982 (despite the close association between FAFERJ and the PMDB) and raised expectations that the party, once in office, would resolve the more pressing and longstanding demands of the urban poor. Brizola's victory also raised expectations among the leadership of the favelas that the party's support of the popular movement meant that the party would be favorable toward popular participation in government.

There is evidence that the PDT has done more for the population of the favelas than any administration to date in Rio, both in terms of its various programs and in terms of the access to the state that the leaders of favela neighborhood associations have enjoyed. The tension between political mobilization and political control remains, however, albeit in a more subtle and somewhat different form.

THE PDT AND THE FAVELAS

The PDT took office in Rio in March of 1983. Soon thereafter the PDT administration unveiled a package of programs targeting the region's favelas. The most important of these programs involved the construction of new public high schools throughout the state. The Centros Integrados de Educação Pública (CIEPs) were designed to keep children in school all day and to provide food, physical recreation, and medical and dental care. A handful of the new schools were actually constructed inside favelas; most, however, were located in close proximity to working-class neighborhoods. And until the program became a political issue in the elections of 1986, it was widely praised as a major step toward the improvement of educational opportunities for the children of the urban poor.

The PDT also developed programs to provide or improve a wide range of basic urban services in the favelas. In its first two years of office, for example, the administration oversaw the installation of water piping in seventy-four favelas and the installation of piped sewage systems in fifty-one favelas. It also conducted a variety of other small-scale public works projects such as the construction of rainfall drainage systems and containing walls, the provision of trash collection, and the installation of public lighting. The Brizola administration also took initial steps toward granting certain favelas the legal right of occupation such that, by September 1985, the state had distributed approximately 13,000 titles of ownership. Finally, a small number of favelas were singled out for special attention, involving considerable financial investment and the participation of a large number of different state agencies. The favelas that benefited most from this were Pavão/Pavãozinho and Cantagalo, two communities in the southern part of the city of Rio.[46]

The PDT administration's style of intervention in the favelas was also very different from that of its predecessors. Investments in the favelas were made by the various state and municipal agencies under the direct control of the executive via universalistic entitlement programs that allocated resources according to social need, not political favoritism. Participation in these programs did not, therefore, depend on the intervention of politicians affiliated with the PDT. During the era of the MDB under Chagas Freitas, gaining access to state agencies responsible for carrying out public works projects had been extremely difficult for favela leaders. This was because access to the state was itself a valued commodity and a source of considerable political power. The PDT, by way of contrast, was a highly centralized party with a very different political structure. Political power within the PDT was concentrated in the hands of the executive and the various state and municipal secretaries, and popular access to these secretaries was relatively open.

This does not mean, however, that the PDT's relationship with the population of the favelas was not designed to serve specific political purposes. In targeting the favelas, the PDT was seeking to undermine one of the principal bases of the PMDB's political power in the region, a goal that it pursued by means of fairly traditional political tactics. An essential aspect of the PDT's strategy was to carry out public works projects in a small but highly visible part of the largest possible number of favelas in Rio. In most cases, these projects would also be carried out in stages. The rationale behind this strategy was twofold. First, these projects, no matter how small, would in themselves generate substantial support for the party. Second, conducting these projects in stages encouraged those who might have voted otherwise to vote for the PDT, for fear that the projects would be discontinued if the party was not returned to office.[47]

Thus, while the style of the PDT's intervention in the favelas differed from that of previous administrations, it was, in essence, no more than a subtle form of clientelism. The PDT, like the PMDB before it, was looking to establish a captive and docile clientele in the favelas by milking the association between politics and public works. The only difference between the tactics employed by the PDT and the tactics employed by the PMDB was that in the case of the PDT the association between public works and political support was not so obvious. Thus, while the PDT was committed to the idea of improving conditions in the favelas, the motivation behind the party's strategy was always the mobilization of votes. And public works, while not directly associated with elections, were still represented as "favors" that, according to popular custom, deserved to be rewarded at the ballot box.

A second and equally important aspect of the PDT's strategy in Rio was its co-optation of the favela leadership. In opening the corridors of the state and municipal administrations to the leadership of the favelas, the PDT created the impression that it was not only favorable toward, but in fact encouraged, popular participation in the decision-making process. This impression was made all the more convincing by the fact that the PDT filled the corridors of the SMDS with the presidents of favela neighborhood associations, ostensibly to work as advisors to state agencies responsible for implementing the party's programs.

The PDT's tactics represented something of a dilemma for the leadership of the favela movement in Rio. For while it applauded the PDT's commitment to the urban poor, it was equally aware of the fact that the administration's relationship with the population of the favelas made it difficult for even the more organized and politically experienced leaders of the favela movement to maintain their independence from the party. Nowhere was this dilemma more obvious than in the relationship that developed between the PDT and FAFERJ.

In April 1985 elections were held for a new president and directorate of FAFERJ. In these elections the incumbent president and directorate were opposed by and lost to a coalition of favela leaders supported by the PDT, PT, PMDB, and the Pastoral de Favelas. This coalition had been organized to protest the incumbent president's attempts to subordinate FAFERJ's interests to those of a radical political faction within the PMDB. The PDT showed a keen interest in developing a relationship with the new directorate and was quick to offer its political and financial support. Within a year, all but one or two of the new directors of FAFERJ who were not openly supportive of the PDT's policies had been expelled from the federation. The result was that criticism of the Brizola administration within FAFERJ was effectively stifled, a situation that led other favela leaders to accuse the new directors of FAFERJ of compromising the federation's political autonomy, much as their predecessors had before them.[48]

The leadership of FAFERJ's relationship with the PDT was not without its complications, however. First of all, it was extremely difficult for the leaders of FAFERJ to take issue with an administration that was investing so much time and money in the favelas and that was already extremely popular among the urban poor. Second, as a federation of favelas, FAFERJ commanded few material resources. This made it almost totally dependent on the patronage of the local state. FAFERJ's administrative offices were located in a building in downtown Rio that was leased, rent-free, from the municipal government, and a number of the directors of FAFERJ were also employed part-time by the PDT as political advisors. Finally, it was not uncommon for directors of FAFERJ to be granted much-disputed nominations as candidates for the PDT in local elections.

The dangers involved in FAFERJ's relationship with the PDT did not go unnoticed, however. Indeed, most if not all of the directors of FAFERJ were aware of the PDT's intentions and expressed at least the desire to prevent FAFERJ from becoming a cabo eleitoral for Brizola. The president of FAFERJ himself told me that "like all political parties the PDT is interested in popular participation only up to a certain point; what it is really interested in is the domination and control of social movements."[49]

Of course, no political party is monolithic, even one as centralized and autocratic as the PDT. And the relationship between FAFERJ and the PDT improved somewhat with the election of Roberto Saturnino Braga as mayor of Rio de Janeiro in November 1985.[50] Braga was a prominent member of the socialist Left of the PDT and was one of the few politicians with sufficient prestige to stand up to Brizola. Braga was also more open to the idea of popular participation in government, so much so that he chose the ex-president of the federation of middle-class neighborhood associations, the Federação de Associações de Moradores do Estado do Rio de Janeiro (FAMERJ),[51] as his running mate, despite considerable opposition from within the ranks of the PDT.

Once in office, Braga authored a series of initiatives designed to establish a new relationship between his self-declared socialist government and the population at large. The most heralded of these initiatives was the creation of local government/community councils that were to determine priorities for state investment in each of Rio's twenty-three RAs. When the idea of the government/community councils was first announced, it appeared that they were to be headed by democratically elected administrators. Later on, however, Braga shied away from the idea of free elections and restricted participation to those who were already card-carrying members of the PDT. One of the directors of FAFERJ had this to say about the project:

> It's clear that we know that all the time, whatever position the government takes is political. Therefore, it is clear that the government, in its term of office, is working all the time to prepare a structure for the elections, because it wants to strengthen the party to which it belongs in a number of ways. One of these ways is this council and the direct elections for the regional administrator. In reality it is not a total opening [*abertura*] and it's not this that we want. We understand that before the existence of political

parties exist people and proposals, and this has to be respected. They're not respecting people as people but as objects for use.[52]

Conclusion

The favelas of Rio have been targets of state repression since they first emerged on the city's hillsides at the beginning of this century. State repression has been tempered, however, by the desire of local political elites to exploit the misery and uncertainty of favela life. This means that, at different times since the establishment of popular democracy and extension of the franchise in the mid 1940s, many politicians and candidates for public office in Rio have come to rely on the favelas as a cheap and readily available source of votes.

The mobilization of support among the population of Rio's favelas has not been without cost, however, in that it has provided both the opportunities and the resources for the political participation and organization of the urban poor. And while the political participation and organization of the urban poor in Rio continue to reflect the actions and decisions of local political elites, they have also been shaped by the various strategies that have been adopted by the residents of Rio's favelas themselves. An analysis of these various strategies is considered in the remaining chapters.

2

RAISING THE STAKES

Neighborhood Politics in Vila Brasil

It is a widely held belief that the favelas of Rio house an unorganized and largely ignorant population that is easy prey for those who would exploit the misery and uncertainty of favela life. Nothing could be further from the truth, however. Over the years, the population of the favelas has learned to participate in politics in ways that have significantly increased its share of the spoils. This chapter tells the story of the favela of Vila Brasil, a favela whose participation in the political process represents a calculated and pragmatic response to prevailing political opportunities, both past and present. It reveals the underlying and compelling logic of clientelist politics and explains why the urban poor so readily participate in rituals that appear to run counter to their long-term interests.

The Favelas of Zona Oeste

Vila Brasil is located in the neighborhood of Magalhães Bastos, approximately fifteen miles due west of the center of Rio and a few miles from the industrial district of Bangu. Together, the RAs of Bangu, Campo

TABLE 5
Favela Population of Zona Oeste and Bangu, 1980

Region	Favela Population	% of Total Regional Population	% of Total Municipal Favela Population
Bangu	51,821	10	7
Zona Oeste	70,849	7	10
Municipality	722,424	14	100

SOURCE: IPLANRIO, *Contribuição aos Dados de População das Favelas do Município do Rio de Janeiro* (Rio de Janeiro: IPLANRIO, 1984), p. 6.

Grande, and Santa Cruz form an area of the municipality of Rio de Janeiro known locally as Zona Oeste (Western Zone). Zona Oeste extends westward from the outskirts of the middle-class suburbs of Tijuca along the railroad tracks and roadways that link the city to the interior of the state of Rio and to neighboring São Paulo.

Zona Oeste is without a doubt one of the poorest areas of Rio. And yet, we see from Table 5 that a relatively small percentage of its population (7 percent) lives in favelas. This is because a large number of the region's poor live in the now-crumbling public-housing projects constructed in the 1960s and 1970s to accommodate families that were removed from favelas in and around the city center, or in the ever-increasing number of illegal subdivisions that have become such a prominent feature of the region.[1]

Table 6 reveals that, consistent with other areas of the city, the vast majority of the favelas in Zona Oeste are small settlements of less than 2,000 people. There are, however, fewer large favelas or favela agglomerations in Zona Oeste than elsewhere in Rio. The two exceptions are the favelas of Vila do Vintém (population 15,877) and Fazenda Coqueiro (population 14,115), both located in the neighborhood of Bangu.[2]

The most noticeable difference between the favelas of Zona Oeste and those in other parts of the city, however, is their physical appearance. The favelas of Zona Oeste are settled on a vast expanse of recently developed, relatively flat land that boasts few areas of up-market housing. They are, therefore, very different from the favelas that cling to the

TABLE 6
Favelas of Zona Oeste and Bangu
by Population Size, 1980

Population	Bangu (22 Favelas)	Zona Oeste (44 Favelas)	Municipality (376 Favelas)
<500	46%	43%	42%
501–2000	27	36	34
2001–5000	18	16	14
>5001	9	5	10
Total	100	100	100

SOURCE: IPLANRIO, *Contribuição aos Dados de População das Favelas do Município do Rio de Janeiro* (Rio de Janeiro: IPLANRIO, 1984), pp. 14–31.

near-vertical hillsides of the city center or the sprawling, densely packed agglomerations of favelas of the industrial districts of northern Rio. Furthermore, the favelas of Zona Oeste have also, until recently, been most deprived of a whole range of basic urban services. Historically, the few programs that have targeted the favelas have affected those in and around the wealthier residential districts and the city center, where the proximity of large concentrations of the urban poor has been perceived as a physical and psychological threat. The favelas of Zona Oeste are located far from such areas and, as a consequence, are perhaps the worst served of all the favelas in the municipality of Rio.[3]

The Political Context of Zona Oeste

Zona Oeste is a region of particular political interest. First, it disposes of well over a half a million votes, or 7 percent of the voting population of the entire state. Second, it is a region where ideological discourse in politics is most noticeable by its absence and where the most effective mechanism for the mobilization of political support among the urban poor has been the promise of employment, a truckload of cement, or, perhaps, a set of shirts for the local soccer team.

When Zona Oeste was first settled as a residential suburb of Rio in the

1940s and 1950s, politics in the region was dominated by a small number of powerful, locally based families. By the mid 1970s, however, the influence of these families had begun to wane or had been assimilated by the political machine of Antônio de Pádua Chagas Freitas and the Movimento Democrático Brasileiro (MDB). This meant that by the mid 1970s, each region of Zona Oeste was under the personal political control of a single Chaguista boss. These bosses were elected to office almost solely on the basis of votes that they commanded in their respective areas of jurisdiction, votes they subsequently delivered in support of the party leadership. In fact, it was in Zona Oeste that two-time governor Chagas Freitas enjoyed his highest levels of political support.[4]

In 1982, the same politicians whose control over the region had once seemed so secure were unceremoniously thrown from office in the wake of the victory of Leonel Brizola and his newly formed Partido Democrático Trabalhista (PDT). Brizola amassed a staggering 170,831 votes in Zona Oeste, as opposed to only 53,303 by Partido Democrático Social (PDS) candidate Wellington Moreira Franco, and a measly 44,787 by the handpicked successor to Chagas Freitas, Partido do Movimento Democrático Brasileiro (PMDB) candidate Miro Teixeira. The returns for the elections for representatives to the Senate, Federal House of Representatives, and State Assembly from the region proved equally disastrous for the PMDB. Then, in the elections for a new mayor of the city of Rio in November 1985, Zona Oeste once again voted overwhelmingly in favor of the PDT. Fully 56 percent of all votes in Bangu and 54 percent of all votes in Campo Grande were cast for PDT candidate Roberto Saturnino Braga such that, together, these two areas presented the PDT with its highest concentration of votes in the entire municipality. The PMDB candidate and local Chaguista boss, Jorge Leite, on the other hand, was beaten into a very poor third place, even in those areas long considered his personal political domain.

Successive electoral defeats suffered by the PMDB at the hands of the PDT in 1982 and 1985 were interpreted, at the time, as evidence that the population of Zona Oeste had tired of clientelism and that the style of politics that had once been the foundation of Chaguista power in the region was no longer an effective electoral strategy. Incredibly, therefore, it appeared that the region had gone from being the redoubt of

Chaguismo to being the redoubt of Brizolismo in the space of just four years.[5]

This sudden and dramatic change in the political morphology of Zona Oeste was aided and abetted by the presence of one of only two active regional Federação de Associações de Favelas do Estado do Rio de Janeiro (FAFERJ) organizations in Rio de Janeiro.[6] Following a lengthy period of dormancy, the regional organization of FAFERJ in Zona Oeste was reactivated in the early 1980s by militants from the Partido dos Trabalhadores (PT), a local Irish priest, and agents from the Pastoral de Favelas. It was primarily concerned with challenging popular perceptions of the political process and with encouraging alternative forms of leadership in the favelas. This meant explaining to the presidents of local neighborhood associations that it was ultimately to their disadvantage to exchange votes for favors, a practice that, for many of them, had become almost second nature. It also meant showing the leaders of individual favelas how to organize delegations that could take the neighborhood association's demands in person to the various government agencies downtown.

The Pastoral de Favelas and the regional FAFERJ organization enjoyed a measure of success in raising levels of popular participation in the favelas of Zona Oeste and were largely responsible for the rapid increase in the number of neighborhood associations in the area in the early 1980s. The extent to which they succeeded in changing the nature of favela politics in the region is less than clear, however. In 1982 the regional leadership of FAFERJ made a tactical decision to persuade local favela leaders to support Brizola's candidacy for governor. This decision was made in the knowledge that victory for the PDT would have both its advantages and disadvantages. On the one hand, victory for the PDT in Zona Oeste would inflict telling damage to political forces associated with Chagas Freitas. On the other hand, victory for the PDT would expose the population of the region's favelas to a different and more sophisticated threat to popular participation.

This concern proved to be well founded. Soon after taking office in 1983 the Brizola administration solicited the advice of favela leaders in Zona Oeste in drawing up plans for a wide range of public works projects. These projects were designed to create the impression that the

PDT was rewarding the population of the favelas for the large number of votes that the party's candidates had received in the region. More important, however, the public works projects made it far more difficult for leaders associated with FAFERJ and the Pastoral de Favelas in Zona Oeste to convince the presidents of neighborhood associations that Brizola was playing an old and familiar game. One of the regional directors of FAFERJ, who was also a local agent for the Pastoral de Favelas, explained the situation:

> The difference is that Brizolismo is more sophisticated. Chaguismo was clearly clientelistic, even explicitly so. With Brizolismo it's not so explicit. The movement is unable to recognize that it's the same thing. Chagas Freitas would never talk to the favela movement. Not so with Brizola. He calls you to talk, promises and even does certain things. But it's the same old clientelism, a lot more sophisticated since you appear to emphasize popular participation. In reality you are being called to be consulted, but never to make or to have an influence on decisions. In effect, although community participation has been good up to a certain point, we have not been part of, or privy to, the global political scheme of the administration's program.[7]

The Brizola administration also made a concerted effort to undermine the authority of the more experienced and independent-minded leaders of the favela movement in Zona Oeste. One leader recounted the story of the day his neighborhood threw a party to celebrate the inauguration of a public works project that was the result of much hard work by local residents. He told me that in the early hours of the morning, a coachload of PDT militants descended on the favela with leaflets claiming that the project was, in essence, a gift from the PDT. Apparently, this was typical of the administration's attempts to discredit the work of neighborhood association presidents who refused to toe the party line.

The PDT was not the only party involved in the conspiracy to silence the more independent and vocal elements of the favela movement in Zona Oeste, however. Following the election of a new president and directorate of FAFERJ in 1985, the Zona Oeste branch of the federation found itself under increasing pressure from the executive in downtown Rio to establish a closer relationship with the PDT. To be fair to the PDT, however, it should be pointed out that, for whatever reason, the PDT did honor its pledge to divert public resources toward the improvement of basic urban services in the region, such that by July 1985 the administration had initiated projects to install piped water systems in thirteen favelas and piped sewage systems in thirty-six favelas in Zona Oeste.[8]

The Favela of Vila Brasil

Vila Brasil (Map 2) stands on a flat, 37,000-square-meter plot of land in the middle of a poor, nondescript, working-class neighborhood. When it was first settled in the 1940s, the areas on either side of the favela were open and semirural. With time and the westward expansion of Rio, however, the neighborhood has become increasingly densely populated. Vila Brasil has also grown considerably over the past forty years, such that today almost all available land in the favela has been enclosed and built upon. In fact, most plots in the favela now boast more than a single dwelling and, in many cases, what at first sight appears to be a single household is often subdivided into as many as seven or eight different units. The favela continues to expand, however, as more families add on a second or third floor. Unlike favelas nearer the city center, however, the majority of the houses in Vila Brasil are still single-story constructions.

Vila Brasil is dissected by three narrow roads that are accessible by vehicle. On either side of these roads are a succession of small stores, workshops, and bars. From these roads sprout a labyrinth of alleyways that weave their way into the heart of the slum. No one knows how many people live in the favela. By the neighborhood association's own calculations there were 524 houses in the favela in 1986. This means that the population of the favela was somewhere in the region of 2,700. Thus, while not one of Rio's largest favelas, Vila Brasil is by no means one of its smallest.[9]

From Table 7 we see that Vila Brasil is a relatively stable and unchanging community in that the majority of the adult population has lived in the favela for more than twenty years and that only a small proportion

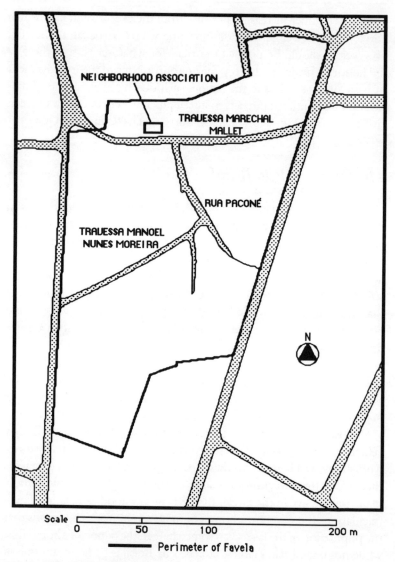

NEIGHBORHOOD ASSOCIATION

TRAVESSA MARECHAL MALLET

RUA PACONÉ

TRAVESSA MANOEL NUNES MOREIRA

N

Scale
0   50   100   200 m

——— Perimeter of Favela

MAP 2. *The Favela of Vila Brasil*

TABLE 7
Length of Residence and Highest Year of Schooling of the Adult Population of Vila Brasil, 1986

Years of Residence		Highest Level of Schooling	
0–10	10.2%	None	13.4%
11–20	23.6	Primary school incomplete	42.5
21+	66.2	Primary school complete	33.1
		Secondary school incomplete	7.1
		Secondary school complete	3.9

NOTE: Data in this table were collected as part of a 1986 survey of political preferences (presented in more detail in Chapter 5). Since the survey was interested primarily in the voting habits of the adult population of Vila Brasil, no data were collected for residents under the age of eighteen.

has moved there in the past decade. Table 7 also reveals that the majority of the adult population (55.9 percent) failed to complete primary school and that a substantial number of adults in the favela have never attended school.

All but a few of the residents of Vila Brasil work for a living, the vast majority in the service sector.[10] The male residents work in a wide variety of occupations, as mechanics, masons, carpenters, overnight watchmen, leather workers, machine operators, electricians, and shopkeepers. There are also a few soldiers living in the favela. Nearly 50 percent of the women work at home as housewives. A further 15 percent work as domestic servants, and a small but significant percentage (about 7 percent) generate extra income by selling candy and handicrafts from stalls in front of their homes. Others work as nurses, teachers, waitresses, and cashiers. Many of these jobs are located in the vicinity of the favela. It is not uncommon, however, for the residents of Vila Brasil to travel two hours by bus Monday through Saturday to minimum-wage jobs in the city center.

The most striking feature of Vila Brasil is that it does not fit the traditional stereotype of a slum in Rio. In fact, it looks less like a slum than many of the surrounding neighborhoods do, such is the general lack of basic urban services in the region. It is only when you enter individual households or walk around the heart of the favela that you confront the poverty and cramped conditions popularly associated with slum life. All but a few households in Vila Brasil are built out of bricks and mortar, all are connected to piped water and piped sewage systems, and each has its own light meter. The roads and alleyways are paved with asphalt and all are well lit at night. The favela also boasts a large and well-maintained neighborhood association building and an equally impressive recreational area for children. In fact, in terms of physical infrastructure, there is little doubt that Vila Brasil is one of the best-served favelas in the area. This has not always been the case, however. Indeed, just ten years ago Vila Brasil had no public lighting, no water supply, and no paved roads, and raw sewage ran through the favela in open ditches. So what accounts for this sudden and dramatic transformation?

The transformation of Vila Brasil is in part a consequence of changes in the macropolitical environment. Political liberalization since the mid 1970s has meant that the more authoritarian solutions to the problem of the favelas in Rio have been set aside in favor of attempts to build a measure of support among the urban poor. This means that in this time the favelas have benefited more from state handouts than at any time in the past. Political liberalization has also meant an increase in the level of political competition. Gone is the two-party system created by the military; in its place is one that in Rio in 1986 sported no less than twenty-eight different political parties. This meant approximately two thousand candidates running for 119 elected offices. It is largely the manipulation of the opportunities provided by political competition that explains Vila Brasil's spectacular success vis-à-vis other favelas in the area.

Political Organization in Vila Brasil

Like most favelas in Rio, Vila Brasil is a closely knit community.[11] The center of the community is, without doubt, the neighborhood association. The only other organization of note in the favela is the local samba block. The samba block plays an important role in the social, cultural, and political life of the favela. It enjoys nothing like the prestige or influence of the neighborhood association, however.[12]

Of the 524 individual households in Vila Brasil in 1986, approximately 300 were affiliated with the neighborhood association. To be a member, each household is required to pay a nominal monthly fee, although households that fall behind in their payments and households that refuse to join are in no way prohibited from using the services that the neighborhood association provides. Membership dues pay the president's expenses, the costs of running the neighborhood association, and the wages of one full-time secretary.

The neighborhood association also counts on a board of nine elected directors, whose job is to assist the president, and a team of three fiscal monitors, who evaluate the president and directorate's performance at the end of each year. In reality, however, the neighborhood association in Vila Brasil is run almost single-handedly by the current president, who, while lamenting the fact that no one is willing to help, revels in the authority and influence his position affords him.

The neighborhood association performs a wide range of social and educational functions in the favela. The most important of these is the administration of two educational programs, one a state-sponsored literacy program for 60 students, the other a municipal nursery school program for 150 children between the ages of three and six. Political functions in the favela are extremely rare. When meetings are held, the population of the favela is more often than not summoned so that it can be informed of decisions that the president of the neighborhood association has already made. As a result, there is little organized political debate in Vila Brasil, and political participation is kept to a minimum. No one thinks of challenging the president's methods or his monopoly of the decision-making process, however, as long as he continues to improve the quality of life in the favela.[13]

While the favela of Vila Brasil has existed in its present site since 1946, the first neighborhood association was not founded until 1952. By all accounts, however, the first president of the neighborhood association did little to further the community's interests. In fact, he took possession of the neighborhood association building, opened up a public bar and poolroom, and never in his twenty-seven years of office called an election.

The first president of the neighborhood association also expressed little interest in politics except when candidates came looking for votes. On such occasions he would agree to campaign for candidates in the understanding that the neighborhood association would be rewarded if the candidate was elected to public office. More often than not, however, the candidate failed to be elected or claimed that he or she received too few votes in the favela. Either way, the president and the favela ended up with nothing.

The situation finally came to a head in 1979, when a group of local residents, with the support of the Pastoral de Favelas, took the president to court to have him evicted from the neighborhood association's property. According to one of those present at the hearing, the judge, on seeing a crowd of favelados in his courtroom, immediately ruled in favor of the plaintiffs. Soon after this decision, elections were held for a new president and directorate of the neighborhood association. The winner was the current president, with a two-thirds majority. The same individual ran and won again by a large margin in 1982 and was reelected, this time without opposition, as president in 1984. Today there is no visible opposition to his leadership.

Now in his sixties, the current president of the neighborhood association left his native city of Natal in the Northeast of Brazil at the age of nine. On arrival in Rio, he found his first job selling combs and pens from a roadside stall in one of the public squares in Rio's docklands. From there he moved to the docks themselves, working as a stevedore for thirty-two years.[14] Uneducated and functionally illiterate, he values the lessons learned during his many years working the streets more than anything a formal education might have taught him.

Since taking over the neighborhood association in 1979, the president has used his considerable acumen to cultivate a network of friends and contacts in the various government agencies and political-party offices in downtown Rio. The president's relationship with politicians and administrators is based on his understanding of elite attitudes toward the urban poor. By playing the role of the humble and ignorant favelado,

A rooftop view of Vila Brasil facing south

One of Vila Brasil's three main roads

The president of Vila Brasil outside the neighborhood association

A roadside bar in Vila Brasil

A typical alleyway in Vila Brasil

the president knows that he has a good chance of receiving favorable treatment. Therefore, at meetings, the president is always the one to take the administrator or politician aside, to greet him warmly, to compliment him, to shake his hand, and so on. He is always careful not to appear aggressive or intransigent.[15]

It is written in the statutes of every neighborhood association that the organization cannot be used as a tool of party politics. This means that in their capacity as leaders of neighborhood associations presidents and directors should not declare themselves in favor of any party or candidate. The president of Vila Brasil agrees in principle with this clause, even if he has not always abided by it. In fact, between 1982 and 1985 the president of the neighborhood association worked as a cabo eleitoral for local-based politician Leite, one of the more powerful figures among the group of politicians associated with Chagas Freitas within the PMDB. Leite was first elected to public office in 1978 as a representative to Rio's State Assembly. In 1982 he ran as a candidate for a seat in the Federal House of Representatives in Brasília.

Leite is the classic clientelist politician. Over the years he has used his access to public resources as an elected official to create and maintain an extensive network of friends and followers. According to the president of Vila Brasil, Leite has no interest in talking about politics. His sole concern is in guaranteeing sufficient votes to ensure his reelection. Until the PMDB's defeat at the hands of Brizola and the PDT in 1982, Leite had the means to do this, his political influence stretching far from his traditional power base in Madureira to the farthest-flung regions of Zona Oeste.

The president of the neighborhood association was first approached by one of Leite's cabos prior to the elections in 1982. Initial contact was made when the president prevented Leite's campaign workers from distributing the candidate's campaign publicity in Vila Brasil. Having observed the past leadership's inability to take advantage of the opportunities presented by clientelist politics, the president let it be known that only those who did something for the community *before* the election would be allowed to campaign in the favela. This challenge initiated a process of intense negotiation between the president and individuals close to Leite, culminating in a visit to Vila Brasil by the candidate himself. It was then that the association between the president and Leite began.

After much discussion, the president of the neighborhood association agreed to work as Leite's cabo eleitoral in Vila Brasil. The president was to be responsible for distributing Leite's campaign publicity to each house in the favela and for hanging campaign posters where they could easily be seen. Though strictly illegal, the president also erected on the roof of the neighborhood association a huge campaign banner bearing Leite's name, making it clear that the candidate enjoyed the neighborhood association's full support. Most important of all, however, the president used his own position of authority in the favela to persuade people to vote for "his" candidate and for the PMDB candidate for governor, Teixeira. In return, every one of the favela's roads and alleyways were paved in the eight days leading up to the November 15 elections. Leite also sent truckloads of sand and cement to assist in the reconstruction of the neighborhood association building.

The election came and went. The PMDB lost the election for governor and, thereby, control of state and municipal government in Rio. Leite, on the other hand, was successful in his bid to be elected to the Federal House of Representatives. Amassing more than 170,000 votes, he was the fifth most popular federal deputy in the state and by far the most voted for among all his colleagues within the PMDB. Leite was not the only one to benefit from this transaction, however. The paving of Vila Brasil also increased the standing and influence in the favela of the president of the neighborhood association. The residents of Vila Brasil understood that he had been personally responsible for an improvement in the quality of their lives that a few years earlier had seemed beyond the realms of all possibility.

The paving of Vila Brasil was, and still is, without doubt the president's finest achievement and an event that secured his position at the head of the neighborhood association for years to come. It was by no means his only success, however. In 1981, for example, the federal government initiated a scheme to install public lighting in the favelas. The program was a popular one, since at the time most favelas relied on illegal and somewhat precarious sources of electricity. By all accounts, the program was also implemented with the minimum of the usual political interference. The president of the neighborhood association was able, nonetheless, to bribe one of the directors of the program with imported whiskey and French perfume to place Vila Brasil's file at the top of the list of favelas that were to benefit from the program.[16] This transaction was made with an eye to the elections in 1982, in the understanding that the president would throw his support behind candidates for the PDS, one of whom just happened to be the program's director.

The more the president manages to achieve for the favela of Vila Brasil and for other communities in the immediate area, the more he is sought after at each election. Candidates know that he commands many votes in the area and that he represents a worthwhile investment of their time and money.[17] The president's ability to get his hands on public resources is not, however, confined to periods of electoral activity. Over the years he has used his considerable skill and his reputation as a political broker to persuade key personnel in a bewildering array of state agencies to channel things his way, sometimes in return for specific favors, but more often than not in the hope that their "friendship" will bear fruit sometime in the not-too-distant future.[18]

Politics in Vila Brasil is, therefore, relatively straightforward and uncomplicated. The president of the neighborhood association is willing to campaign only for candidates who are able to deliver tangible benefits to the community before each election. The relationship between the president of the neighborhood association and individual candidates is, therefore, nakedly transactional. Beyond the dispute in question, the president of the neighborhood association expresses no preference or allegiance to any politician, party, or ideology. The president's strategy is a common one among the leadership of Rio's favelas. It reflects the population of the favela's almost universal disdain for politics, a disdain that is itself the product of almost a century of repression, manipulation, and neglect.[19]

Parties, Politicians, and Political Loyalty

One of the president's favorite sayings is that "politicians are all thieves, but I'm a much better thief than any of them." What he means is that politicians are interested in one thing and one thing only: political power. Political power, according to the president, is one of the few avenues for personal gain in Brazil. Consequently, the vast majority of politicians elected to public office are concerned above all else with lining their own pockets. Politicians claim that they are interested in the plight of the urban poor. In reality, however, they are interested in exploiting the misery and uncertainty of favela life. Knowing this, the president of Vila Brasil takes it upon himself to play politicians at their own game, to exploit their desire for votes when and wherever the opportunity arises.[20]

The president spares no politicians from scorn, whether male or female, rich or poor, or of the Left or Right. In fact, he makes no such distinctions. He is particularly dismissive, however, of politicians who were once favelados themselves. In 1982 two candidates from favelas in Zona Oeste were elected as representatives to the State Assembly on behalf of the PDT.[21] The president claims that these local-based politicians then turned their backs on the favelas. The fact that politicians from the favelas can so readily abandon their natural constituencies is, to the president, proof enough of the corrupting influence of politics.[22]

The president's perception of politicians as a bunch of self-interested, money-grabbing thieves means that he has even less time for political parties. He says that he does not bother keeping track of the constant to and fro of politicians from one party to another, nor does he take an interest in the proliferation of new political parties in Rio. As president of the neighborhood association, he says that his main concern is to take advantage of his contacts with individual politicians and administrators in positions of authority and that he does not care which party they belong to.

Thus, while the president worked on and off for Leite for five years, he expresses no loyalty to the man or his party. Because of the success of their 1982 agreement, however, the president continued working for Leite in the hope that this relationship would bear further fruit. The prospect of further gain appeared especially favorable when Leite was nominated as the PMDB candidate for elections for mayor of Rio in 1985. Leite promised the president that if he supported his candidacy in Vila Brasil he would be rewarded financially and with jobs for his family and children. Neither promises were kept, however.[23] Essentially, Leite expected the president to continue working for him on the basis of what he had done for Vila Brasil in 1982. So, following Leite's disastrous showing in the elections for mayor in 1985, the president decided to terminate their relationship.[24]

The president's decision to break with Leite was governed by three considerations. First, the president had no doubt that it was unwise for him to continue working for someone who was coming off a serious political defeat. True, Leite was still an influential figure within the PMDB, but the party itself had recently lost control of both state and municipal governments in Rio. The PMDB's electoral misfortunes greatly restricted Leite's access to public resources, and public resources represented his principal means of generating votes. Second, the president claimed that his association with Leite was getting in the way of his relationship with the PDT. It appeared that almost everyone who worked for the government knew of his association with Leite to the extent that it was restricting his access to key personnel. This was proving to be a serious impediment for someone who relied so heavily on manipulating personal contacts and the politics of favors. Finally, the PDT had initiated a large number of small public works projects in the favelas of Zona Oeste, including Vila Brasil. The president was very conscious of this fact. It was not that the president viewed the PDT any less unfavorably than he did other political parties but that he had no desire to damage his community's chances of benefiting further.[25]

The relationship of the president of the neighborhood association with the PDT was necessarily quite different from that which he enjoyed with the PMDB. The PDT was organized along very different lines from the PMDB, meaning that there was no one of the likes of Leite for him to work with at the local level, at least no one with the equivalent access to public resources. The PDT also did not make the association between public works and political support as obvious as in the heyday of Chaguismo. This meant that the president had to be more subtle about the way he went about his business. In one way or another, however, he let it be known that if the party failed to do anything for his community, it could not expect to pick up many votes in the area. Therefore, if the specific form of the relationship between the president and the party in power had changed, the essence of the relationship stayed very much the same.

As one can well imagine, the president of Vila Brasil's attitude and methods made him unpopular with those more closely involved with the work of FAFERJ and the Pastoral de Favelas in Zona Oeste. The president was, after all, precisely the kind of leader that the more organized elements of the favela movement were trying so hard to remove.[26] They criticized the president for accepting what to them were nothing more than bribes from unscrupulous politicians, for reinforcing the association between politics and public works among his many followers, and for effectively putting an end to alternative forms of political participation in the favela.

Unfortunately, at least as far as the Pastoral de Favelas and FAFERJ were concerned, the president of Vila Brasil's success in making the most of the situation had made him something of a local hero and role model among the presidents of the region's neighborhood associations, to say nothing of his popularity in his own favela. And for the president of Vila Brasil, the bottom line was the fact that his was one of the best-served favelas in Zona Oeste, and, perhaps, in all of Rio.[27]

Conclusion

Ten years ago, Vila Brasil was a favela much like any other in Rio. Isolated, unorganized, and effectively abandoned by the state, Vila Brasil was easy prey for politicians looking for a cheap source of votes. Then, in 1979, the neighborhood association, for all intents and purposes inactive for the first twenty-seven years of its existence, was taken over by a president who learned to take advantage of Vila Brasil's limited but nonetheless important role in the political process. The president made it known that only those candidates who made good on their promises before the election would receive the neighborhood association's blessing and be allowed to campaign in the favela. The president's insistence on a new relationship with politicians paid almost immediate dividends in that it led to the paving of Vila Brasil prior to the elections in 1982.

The president's success in 1982 firmly established his credentials as a local political broker. Knowing that he commanded a substantial number of votes in the area, administrators, politicians, and future candidates for public office began to see the president as a powerful political ally. The president's success also consolidated his position as the undisputed leader of Vila Brasil. As far as his followers were concerned, the president had been personally responsible for the urbanization of the favela, something that had been beyond the realm of all possibility before he assumed control of the neighborhood association in 1979.

Somewhat ironically, the change in Vila Brasil's fortunes was precipitated by efforts on behalf of FAFERJ and the Pastoral de Favelas to cultivate a new style of leadership in the favelas of Zona Oeste. Instead, the reactivation of the neighborhood association in Vila Brasil gave birth to a more successful and, therefore, more enduring variation on an old and familiar theme. Of particular significance in this regard was the fact that the president's methods called for little or no effort on behalf of a population that shared an almost universal disdain for all things political. At a fundamental level, therefore, the president of Vila Brasil's political philosophy proved to be a far more attractive proposition than that which was being promoted by FAFERJ and the Pastoral de Favelas in Zona Oeste.

3

RESHAPING POLITICAL SPACE

Neighborhood Politics in Vidigal

In this chapter we turn our attention to a favela whose involvement with the popular movement in Rio in the late 1970s provoked a very different response than that which we encountered in Vila Brasil. Before it was faced with the threat of removal from its present site in 1977, the favela of Vidigal was much like any other in Rio in that its fate was in the hands of a local political broker whose concern for the community manifested itself during brief periods of electoral activity. The success of the population of Vidigal in halting the removal process and the favela's subsequent involvement with popular organizations intent on challenging the decision-making power of the authoritarian state sparked the reactivation and reorganization of the neighborhood association and the adoption of a mode of interest representation that is the very antithesis of that of the president of Vila Brasil.

The Favelas of Zona Sul

Vidigal is located in the administrative region (RA) of Lagoa between the neighborhoods of São Conrado and Leblon. Together, the RAs of

TABLE 8

Favela Population of Zona Sul and Lagoa, 1980

Region	Favela Population	% of Total Regional Population	% of Total Municipal Favela Population
Lagoa	43,709	20	6
Zona Sul	64,816	9	9
Municipality	722,424	14	100

SOURCE: IPLANRIO, *Contribuição aos Dados de População das Favelas do Município do Rio de Janeiro* (Rio de Janeiro: IPLANRIO, 1984), p. 6.

Lagoa, Copacabana, and Botafogo form an area of Rio known as Zona Sul (Southern Zone). Zona Sul is very different from other parts of the city in that it is both the commercial and tourist center of Rio. Sandwiched between vast stretches of golden sand and spectacular rock formations, Zona Sul is also home to many of the city's elites.

Historically, Zona Sul has been an area of extensive favela settlement. In 1960, for example, it was home to 33 of a total of 147 favelas then in existence, and in 1967, the RA of Lagoa itself housed the second largest favela population in all of Rio.[1] Many of the favelas that were established early on in Zona Sul were subsequently torn down in the 1960s and 1970s.[2] As a consequence, the favela population of Zona Sul is today relatively small. In fact, Table 8 reveals that only 9 percent of all residents of Zona Sul live in favelas and that this figure represents approximately 9 percent of Rio's total favela population. Table 8 also reveals that the majority of the favela population of Zona Sul is to be found in the RA of Lagoa. This is due, in no small part, to the considerable presence of Rocinha, by far the largest favela in Rio. Rocinha is by no means the only large favela in Zona Sul, however. In fact, Table 9 reveals that in the area there are five favelas other than Rocinha with populations of more than two thousand.

The favelas of Zona Sul are physically very different from those found in other parts of the city. The majority of those that survived the removal process in the 1960s and 1970s were favelas that clung to the

TABLE 9
Favelas of Zona Sul and Lagoa by Population Size, 1980

Population	Lagoa (6 Favelas)	Zona Sul (24 Favelas)	Municipality (376 Favelas)
<500	17%	25.0%	42%
501–2000	33	50.0	34
2001–5000	17	12.5	14
>5001	33	12.5	10
Total	100	100.0	100

SOURCE: IPLANRIO, *Contribuição aos Dados de População das Favelas do Município do Rio de Janeiro* (Rio de Janeiro: IPLANRIO, 1984), pp. 14–31.

near-vertical hillsides that litter the area. Today these favelas provide a stark and chilling contrast to some of the most expensive pieces of real estate in all of Latin America. The favelas of Zona Sul are also different in that, somewhat ironically, they have benefited most from recent attempts to urbanize such areas. Thus, for example, approximately one-third of all public works projects initiated by the Secretaria Municipal de Desenvolvimento Social (SMDS) between 1979 and 1982 targeted favelas in Zona Sul.[3]

The favelas of Zona Sul have also enjoyed their fair share of public works projects since the election of the Partido Democrático Trabalhista (PDT) in November 1982. Two favelas deserve special mention in this context. Pavão/Pavãozinho and Cantagalo are two favelas perched side by side atop hillsides in the neighborhoods of Ipanema and Copacabana. In 1984 heavy rainfall triggered landslides in the favela of Pavão/Pavãozinho, carrying many houses down the hillside and causing many fatalities. The PDT responded by drawing up plans for the state and municipal administrations under its control to transform the two slums into "model favelas." Accordingly, Pavão/Pavãozinho and Cantagalo were to benefit from each of the various programs that the PDT was in the process of developing in the region's favelas, as well as others that were specifically designed for this project. The urbanization of Pavão/Pavãozinho

and Cantagalo subsequently became a symbol of the Brizola administration's commitment to the favela population of Rio.[4]

The Political Context of Zona Sul

As one of the wealthier residential districts of Rio, Zona Sul boasts a
particularly conservative electorate. In the elections for a new mayor
in November 1985, PDT candidate Roberto Saturnino Braga was beaten
into second place in only two of twenty-five electoral districts in the
entire city. Both times Braga was defeated by the candidate for the Partido da Frente Liberal (PFL), both times in Copacabana and Ipanema.
In the other two electoral districts in Zona Sul (Lagoa and Botafogo),
Braga managed to defeat the PFL candidate by only a very narrow margin. Having said this, however, the Left enjoys considerable penetration
in the area: the radical Left among students and intellectuals, the PDT
among the population of the favelas.

Since the elections in 1982, the favelas of Zona Sul have been loyal
supporters of Leonel Brizola and the PDT. Before then they were the undisputed domain of the Partido do Movimento Democrático Brasileiro
(PMDB) and of politicians associated with Antônio de Pádua Chagas
Freitas. As in Zona Oeste, the popularity of the Chaguistas in the favelas of Zona Sul was based on their monopoly and selective distribution
of public goods and services. Until 1982, the Chaguistas' strategy in the
favelas proved highly successful. In the 1978 elections, for example, Chaguista candidates for state deputy captured 90 percent of all votes for
Movimento Democrático Brasileiro (MDB) politicians in the favela of
Rocinha and 94 percent of all votes for the MDB in the favela of Vidigal.[5]
The success of Chaguista candidates for federal deputy in the two favelas was less marked. Nonetheless, in both favelas Chaguista candidates
captured more than 50 percent of the MDB vote, and in both Rocinha
and Vidigal the most popular candidate for federal deputy was Miro
Teixeira, the heir apparent of the Chaguista regime. As in Zona Oeste,
however, the elections in 1982 marked a turning point in the fortunes of
the Chaguistas in the favelas of Zona Sul. In 1982 the population of the
favelas turned its back on its former benefactors, and, once again, the

vote en masse for Brizola and the PDT was widely interpreted as evidence that clientelism in Rio's favelas was a thing of the past.

At present, there is no regional Federação de Associações de Favelas do Estado do Rio de Janeiro (FAFERJ) organization in Zona Sul. The local favela leadership has, however, been active in the affairs of the federation in the past. It formed the nucleus of leaders that oversaw the reorganization of FAFERJ in the late 1970s and was intimately involved in the formation of the multiparty coalition that wrested control of the executive of FAFERJ in 1985. The favela leadership of Zona Sul has only recently withdrawn from FAFERJ, because in its eyes the directorate it helped elect in 1985 began compromising the federation's interest through its relationship with the PDT.

The other influence of note in the favelas of Zona Sul is the Catholic church. The Pastoral de Favelas began its work organizing neighborhood associations in the favelas following the attempted removal of Vidigal in 1977 and was intimately involved in the reorganization of FAFERJ in 1979 and the campaign to elect a more representative and democratic executive of FAFERJ in 1985. As a result, the Pastoral de Favelas has enjoyed a very close relationship with the leadership of the favelas in the area, although its influence over favela politics has been on the decline in recent years.[6]

The Favela of Vidigal

Vidigal (Map 3) clings to the side of a towering rock formation separating Leblon and São Conrado, two of the wealthiest neighborhoods in Rio de Janeiro. Immediately below the favela is the Sheraton Hotel complex, one of the more expensive places to stay in the city. Around the corner is the small and highly exclusive neighborhood of Alto Leblon, home to some of Rio's most extravagant mansions. Perhaps more than any other favela in Zona Sul, therefore, Vidigal is testimony to the inequities of twentieth-century capitalist development in Brazil.

The favela itself stretches from the road that hugs the coastline between Leblon and São Conrado to the base of the cliffs (*dois irmãos*) that dominate the skyline of Ipanema and Leblon, a distance in all of

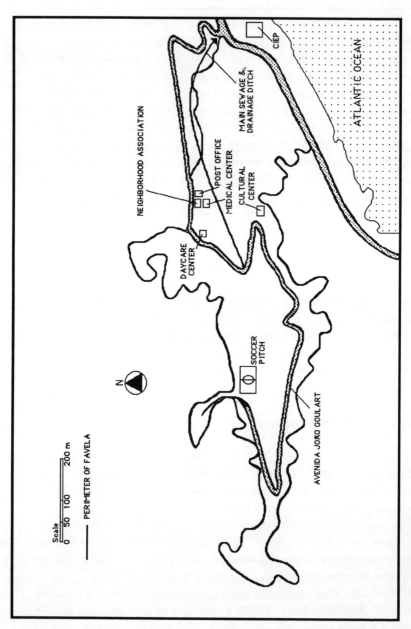

MAP 3. *The Favela of Vidigal*

about one kilometer. At the roadside the houses are built side by side or on top of each other and are accessible only by a maze of narrow and twisting alleyways that weave their way into the heart of the slum. As the favela climbs the hill, the houses become more scattered, until at the very top the favela is quite rural. Only one road in the favela is accessible by vehicle. This road, Avenida João Goulart, serves as the favela's lifeline and winds its way slowly and deliberately up the spine of the hill.

The favela was first settled in 1941 on an area of land between the road that now marks the lower limit of the favela and the ocean sixty feet below. Over the next ten years or so, the favela expanded upward from its original site to its present location between the road and the base of the cliff. In 1950 all of the houses standing below the road were removed. The favela continued to grow, however, engulfing an adjacent slum and taking in residents from favelas removed elsewhere in the city. No one knows how many people live in Vidigal. In 1986 the neighborhood association estimated that the population was somewhere in the region of 9,000. By my own calculation it was around 6,500.[7]

Ten years ago the neighborhood association attempted to halt the expansion of the favela by banning the construction of new houses. Vidigal has continued to grow, however, as families add on a second, third, or even fourth floor and as more houses are converted from wood to brick. There is an air of permanence about the place.

Table 10 reveals that, much like Vila Brasil, the majority of the residents of Vidigal have lived there for some time. There is, however, a considerable degree of turnover in the favela.[8] Table 10 also reveals that, as one might expect, the educational profiles of the two favelas are similar in that a relatively small percentage of the adult population of Vidigal (32.9 percent) completed primary school, and only a select few ever progressed beyond secondary school.

The vast majority of the working population of Vidigal is employed in the service sector in Ipanema, Leblon, and Copacabana or in the business district in downtown Rio.[9] The most common occupations among male residents of the favela are shop assistant (13 percent), bus and taxi driver (9 percent), and doorman (8 percent). A further 13 percent are proprietors of the plethora of stores, bars, and workshops that line the main thoroughfare of the favela or owners of stalls that sell all kinds of

TABLE 10

Length of Residence and Highest Year of Schooling
of the Adult Population of Vidigal, 1986

Years of Residence		Highest Level of Schooling	
0–10	37.5%	None	13.1%
11–20	32.3	Primary school incomplete	54.0
21+	30.2	Primary school complete	25.0
		Secondary school incomplete	3.3
		Secondary school complete	4.6

NOTE: Data in this table were collected as part of a 1986 survey of political preferences (presented in more detail in Chapter 5).

different merchandise in local neighborhood markets. As in Vila Brasil, a significant proportion (42 percent) of the women do no paid work. The most common paid occupation (18 percent) for women is that of domestic servant. The other female occupations of note are seamstress, shop assistant, and a large group of women (10 percent) who described their positions as *diaristas* or *serventes* (day laborers or helpers).

Despite the fact that Vidigal is more than twice the size of Vila Brasil, it too is an extremely close-knit and cohesive favela. The population of Vidigal works together, goes to school together, plays soccer together, organizes and participates in dances and festivals together, and enjoys the Sheraton Hotel's supposedly private beach together. The favela's location adjacent to some of Rio's more expensive pieces of real estate, the physical proximity of its houses, and the sheer size of the population living in such close quarters also contribute a strong sense of community.

Perhaps most important, however, is the sense among the population of the favela that it shares a common and rather unique past. As we shall see, the experiences of the past decade or so have taught the residents of Vidigal the importance of strength in unity and organization. These same experiences have thrust the neighborhood association to the forefront of the political and social life of the favela, a position it maintains to the present day. The neighborhood association in Vidigal is a very different creature from that which we encountered in the favela of Vila Brasil, however.

Political Organization in Vidigal

Vidigal's neighborhood association is highly organized and efficient and is responsible for the provision of a wide range of services in the favela. It is responsible for soliciting state assistance for improvements to the physical infrastructure of the favela and for administrating all public works projects once underway. It is also responsible for the occasional *mutirão*, self-help projects that are organized and, sometimes, financed by the neighborhood association itself. The neighborhood association also administers numerous social services. For example, at present the neighborhood association runs two preschool programs that are financed by the state, and it is responsible for hiring, monitoring, and, if necessary, firing local employees of COMLURB, the municipal garbage collection agency. Finally, the neighborhood association also plays a prominent role in the social life of the favela, from the organization of festivals and dances to excursions to towns in the interior of the state.

At any one time the neighborhood association is run by a directorate of twenty or so volunteers. The directorate consists of a president; a vice-president; three or four secretaries and treasurers; directors of individual departments such as public works, health, and education; and a group of fiscal monitors responsible for evaluating the neighborhood association's performance. Unlike Vila Brasil, presidents of the neighborhood association are prohibited from running for consecutive terms of office, and elections for a new president and directorate are held every two years. These elections are open to the entire adult population of the favela.

The directorate of the neighborhood association convenes twice each week, once on its own and once in an open meeting. At open meetings the directorate reports on any progress or lack thereof in its negotiations with the various municipal, state, and federal government agencies. The directorate also takes advantage of its meetings with the general public to explain and administer the various programs in its charge.[10] Attendance at these meetings varies enormously according to the nature of the business at hand. And although the neighborhood association boasts a dues-paying membership of approximately three thousand, it is rare for more than fifty or sixty to attend on any given day. The neighborhood association's meetings are important, nonetheless, as a source of public information, and those who attend on a regular basis are privy to the intimate details of the neighborhood association's relationship with the state.

The most important distinction between the neighborhood association in Vila Brasil and that in Vidigal lies not in its internal structure but in its relationship with the state and with local political elites. Unlike the neighborhood association in Vila Brasil, that in Vidigal steadfastly refuses to exchange votes for favors. It considers the provision of public services in Vidigal, or in any other favela for that matter, to be a basic right of citizenship and not something that should be purchased or even rewarded at the ballot box. To understand how the leadership of Vidigal came to adopt this position we have to look back at the political history of the favela since it was established some forty years or so ago.

Vidigal and the MDB

For much of its early history, the favela of Vidigal was both isolated and unorganized. In fact, it was only when the favela was periodically threatened with removal that the community was spurred into any form of collective action. The first of such threats occurred in 1958, when the Empresa Industrial Melhoramentos do Brasil tried unsuccessfully to throw the two hundred or so families who were living there off its land. In 1967, the same company tried again. Once again, however, the favela was able to forestall the process. It was this second attempt at removal that sparked the formation of the favela's first neighborhood association, the Associação de Moradores do Vidigal.

Before a year had gone by, however, the neighborhood association was virtually inactive. The favela leadership, to the extent that it existed, had little or no idea how to sustain popular interest in the neighborhood association beyond these periodic crises. As if this were not enough, the military took a dim view of popular organization, and popular access to the state had become even more difficult than before. As a consequence, local interest in the neighborhood association dwindled until it ceased functioning altogether.

With the demise of Vidigal's first neighborhood association came the effective withdrawal of the favela from local political life. As one of the smaller of the ever-increasing number of favelas in Rio, Vidigal enjoyed little contact with members of the local political elite except on the eve of elections, when the usual gaggle of candidates for public office would climb the hill in search of votes. The one politician who did enjoy a degree of popularity in the favela, however, was Paulo Duque.

Duque was the local cog in the MDB political machine. Over the years he managed to construct a sizeable clientele in the favelas of Zona Sul through the selective distribution of patronage. Like others of his genre, Duque took advantage of his access to public funds to make the occasional small donation to a local sports or social club, to nominate certain individuals in his favor to low-level positions in the state and municipal bureaucracies under the MDB's control, and to champion a number of local causes, always with the understanding that those within his geographical jurisdiction would guarantee him and his political superiors their loyal support. Duque's relationship with the favela of Vidigal was much the same. Essentially, Vidigal was "his" favela, despite the fact that he had done little to improve the quality of life in the area.

One of the current directors of the neighborhood association described the relationship between Duque and the favela of Vidigal in the following manner:

> The only politician to visit us regularly and who, therefore, received a good number of votes in the favela was Paulo Duque, who, on reflection, was one of the worst politicians in the entire city of Rio de Janeiro. Here is a guy who, even today, has a following in the favela and who still refuses to talk about politics. These are all people he's arranged work for. If he'd been a good politician, Vidigal would still be his area. At that time even I voted for Paulo Duque.[11]

The relationship between Duque and Vidigal began back in 1974, when a handful of residents decided that something should be done about the provision of electricity in the favela. At the time, the favela received its electricity via an illegal and somewhat precarious hookup to power lines at the bottom of the hill. The only other option that was readily available was the establishment of a comissão de luz. Deciding against this, the residents of Vidigal went instead to see if Duque could help resolve the problem.

Duque claimed that there was little he could do so close to elections in November of that year. Instead, he gave the delegation of residents from Vidigal a set of shirts for the favela's soccer club and promised to take up the issue with the governor after the election, if he was elected. According to one of those who was present at the time, the favela leadership's lack of experience in such matters, the fact that almost nothing could be done without the intervention of a politician, and the fact that the MDB was, for all intents and purposes, the only game in town, meant that many in Vidigal voted for Duque on the basis of this promise alone. Following the election, of course, Duque was nowhere to be found.

In 1977, the specter of removal returned to haunt the favela, but this time in a more determined mood. Between 1967 and 1977 the land upon which the favela stood had been sold twice, the second time to the real estate companies of Rio Towers and Sincorpa. Rio Towers and Sincorpa subsequently drafted plans for the construction of twelve luxury apartment buildings in Vidigal. The ground was to be broken as soon as the favela was removed.[12]

In early October 1977 the residents of Vidigal were informed that the governor of Rio had ordered them removed from their homes and relocated to an apartment complex in Antares, a distant suburb of Santa Cruz. Then, on October 25, representatives from the Fundação Leão XIII, accompanied by military police, appeared at the foot of the favela with instructions to tear down the first houses scheduled for removal. This was to be the initial stage in a process that was to account for the remaining 330 families by January of the following year. The instructions of the Fundação Leão XIII were backed up by threats that the state would cut off all existing supplies of water and electricity to the favela at the first signs of popular resistance.[13]

Conditions in Vidigal were precarious at the time. Few families were willing to invest money in their homes for fear of removal, water and electricity were stolen from official systems adjacent to the favela, and raw sewage and household waste flowed through the neighborhood in open ditches. In spite of this, a number of the residents of the favela decided to ignore the order to leave, a decision that was vindicated when families that had agreed to the move returned from their new homes in Santa Cruz. They had discovered that their new homes were, in many respects, no better than the ones they were being forced to abandon, to say nothing of the fact that the homes were located more than two hours from where most of them worked.[14]

In a desperate attempt to halt the proceedings, a handful of those who had decided against leaving the favela went in search of Duque. This approach met with little success, however. According to one of the current directors of the neighborhood association, Duque refused even to talk to them about the matter. He simply walked by them in the corridor outside his office, gave one of them a reassuring pat on the back, said he was dealing with the problem, and left.

Fortunately, by January of the following year, when most of the houses in Vidigal were scheduled to be torn down, the favela had attracted the sympathy and support of representatives from organizations interested in defending the community's right to remain. These included representatives from the State Assembly and Municipal Chamber in Rio, the Brazilian Institute of Architects, the Brazilian Bar Association, and the Catholic church. Together these organizations and the population of Vidigal challenged the decision to remove the favela. The state claimed that the decision had been made because of the danger of landslides in the area. Everyone knew, however, that it had been motivated by plans to build luxury apartments in Vidigal.[15]

This collective show of force ultimately proved successful in that the state agreed to review its decision to relocate the population of the favela to public-housing projects in Santa Cruz. In celebration, those individuals who were at the forefront of the effort to challenge the removal process ceremoniously reinstated the neighborhood association, dormant for almost a decade, inside the house of one of the few families that had agreed to leave.

Vidigal's success in defending its right to remain was, in itself, a significant popular victory. The vast majority of favelas that were singled out for removal in the 1970s accepted their fate with a degree of inevitability, and those that did offer resistance saw their houses razed to the ground and their leaders beaten and jailed.[16] One of those present at the time pointed out that 1977 "was a time in Brazil when no one said no. Everyone said yes, or yes sir. In 1977 we defended our homes because we had nowhere else to go. We said no. We were the only community that said no. Everyone was afraid to say no. When we said no everyone rallied round us. Now it's difficult to remove favelas."[17]

The events surrounding the attempted eviction of Vidigal represented more than the resistance of a few favelados, however. They were also catalysts for the mobilization of popular resistance to the military in Rio, for subsequent disputes over the control and mandate of FAFERJ, and for the creation of an interventionist and socially conscious Pastoral de Favelas.[18] Most important of all, however, the events surrounding the eviction attempt were responsible for a complete transformation in the political and social life of the favela of Vidigal.

The decision to resist the removal process and the procedure by which the favela overcame this threat to its existence brought what had only recently emerged as the leadership of Vidigal into increasingly close contact with representatives from other communities that were organizing along similar lines. And in fact, much of what the leadership of Vidigal learned from the experiences of 1977 and 1978 was the fruit of its contacts and interactions with leaders from favelas and nongovernment organizations that were more experienced in dealing with the state. Therefore, if the attempt to remove the favela provided the initial spark for the transformation of social and political life in Vidigal, it was the subsequent involvement of the leadership of the favela with popular organizations intent on challenging the decision-making power of the authoritarian state that made this transformation a reality.

Of particular importance in this regard were efforts by the Pastoral de Favelas to cultivate a new generation of leaders that identified with its own work in Rio. The Catholic church played an important part in challenging and eventually halting the eviction process in Vidigal and subsequently took a number of those who had assumed the leadership of the favela under its wing. These individuals went on to form the nucleus of the leadership of the newly reinstated neighborhood association in

Vidigal and to become important players in the Pastoral de Favelas itself and, later on, in the executive administration of FAFERJ.

A New Political Philosophy

Without doubt, the most important lesson that the leadership of Vidigal learned from the attempt to remove the favela was that both the politicians and the political methods it had relied on in the past were largely ineffectual. The leadership came to realize that while Duque was more than willing to make the occasional small donation to the soccer club, he was concerned for the welfare of the population of the favela only to the extent that it would vote for him come election time. The leadership also came to realize that Duque's concern for the favela was certainly not such that he was prepared to risk his relationship with the state administration over the fate of a handful of makeshift wooden huts.

Of course, this was by no means the first time that representatives from Vidigal had gone to Duque to ask for help and had come away empty-handed—far from it. In the past, however, the leaders of the favela had for all intents and purposes been denied any alternative course of action, such that politicians who agreed to talk to them, let alone entertain their demands, appeared to be doing them a massive favor. This time things were different in that the leadership's failure to enlist Duque's support was more than compensated for by the advice it received from fellow favelados, lawyers, journalists, politicians, and priests. This advice was that it was morally reprehensible for anyone to have to beg for things that, in most countries, would be considered basic rights of citizenship.

The outcome of the many conversations between the leadership of Vidigal and its various allies was that the newly reinstated neighborhood association changed the way it went about its business. Instead of pandering to the interests of the more traditional-minded elements of the political class in the hope that they would intervene on the favela's behalf, the leadership of Vidigal decided instead to take its demands directly to the state agencies that were supposedly responsible for the welfare of the favelas in Rio. And, in fact, 1977 marked the last time that the favela, as a body, solicited help from politicians who were looking to exchange votes for favors.[19] As one of the directors of the neighborhood association put it: "We completely cut ourselves off from politicians. Today, I can even say that Vidigal is completely independent of politicians. We take our demands directly to the administrative organs. Because of this, we may even encounter some difficulty in getting certain public works done because, unhappily, politicians are a disgrace."[20]

As this quotation suggests, the leadership of the newly reinstated neighborhood association was not unaware that its decision to depart from the traditional script was a brave one at a time when politicians played a critical role as intermediaries between the state and the population at large. Its decision meant, among other things, that instead of going cap in hand to beg for the occasional favor from the likes of Duque, the neighborhood association would be forced to make its presence felt in the corridors of the various government offices downtown. It was obvious from the start, therefore, that the neighborhood association's success would depend, to a large extent, on the support of the population of Vidigal and the leadership's ability to persuade enough people to participate in the running of the favela.

The leadership's attempts to involve people in the day-to-day administration of the neighborhood association met with considerable resistance, however. Few were willing to give up what little free time they had on weekends or to attend meetings on weekday evenings having worked eight, nine, or ten hours at their regular jobs, so those already involved in the neighborhood association found themselves doing the lion's share of the work. More damaging, however, was the concern expressed by many that the neighborhood association's decision to ignore conventional political wisdom would cost the favela dearly. It was obvious, therefore, that Duque and those like him still commanded a large following in the favela and that there was no shortage of individuals who thought it risky for the neighborhood association to turn its back on its longtime benefactor.

The concern among some residents that the neighborhood association was illadvised in its decision to sever its contacts with Duque was compounded by the more general fear that representatives from the favela would, as a consequence of this decision, be denied access to the state. For as long as anyone could remember, politicians like Duque had effectively controlled who got what, when, and where in Rio. It appeared highly unlikely, therefore, that a handful of favelados who were attempting to cut out the all important middleman would be treated with anything but hostility.

The essential problem was that, despite all that had happened in the past two years, many people still believed that the favela's interests would be best served by pledging its allegiance to the political party in power and that there was neither wisdom nor logic to the neighborhood association's efforts to withdraw from politics, at least in the sense that most people understood it. Before they could do anything else, therefore, the leaders of the neighborhood association and their allies in the church had to convince those who criticized their methods that theirs was indeed a better way.

This meant convincing those who understood the logic of clientelist politics that a neighborhood association that was closely identified with a politician or political party was as much a liability as an asset, since both politicians and political parties could be voted out of office. The best strategy, therefore, would be for the neighborhood association to organize itself and pursue its demands in a way that was largely independent of party politics. As one of the directors of the neighborhood association of the time explained to me: "We don't try and stay outside of politics; we stay within politics. We have people from every party. This is important. A neighborhood association cannot be affiliated with a particular party. If you support a certain government and party, and that party loses, you will have great difficulty afterwards in getting things done for your community."[21]

The decision to keep party and neighborhood association politics separate meant that instead of thinking of the vote as a form of political downpayment or reward, the leadership of the neighborhood association was asking the population of Vidigal to vote for politicians and political parties that were concerned not only with the more immediate, day-to-day concerns of the favela but also with the more general issues of education, health care, and wages. This did not mean that the leaders of the neighborhood association considered the provision of sewers, roads, and electricity as any less important, but that the pursuit of the favela's more immediate demands should follow a different political logic.

Essentially, the leaders of the neighborhood association maintained that all administrations, regardless of political ideology, had a duty to address problems associated with the lack of urban services in the favela and that as basic rights of citizenship such things were not necessarily worthy of support. The leaders of the neighborhood association were, therefore, asking the residents of Vidigal to entrust them with the task of improving the physical infrastructure of the favela while they focused their attention on a series of other, nonetheless related, issues that were beyond the neighborhood association's influence and control.[22]

The rationale behind this strategy was that while the benefits to be accrued from cuddling up to politicians often made life a little easier, they were *always* given in the understanding that they would be rewarded at the ballot box. Therefore, by addressing some of the more minor symptoms of urban poverty, politicians could not only guarantee a measure of political support but also deflect popular attention away from other more general issues affecting the urban poor. As a two-time president of the neighborhood association explained to me:

> You don't have to vote for a politician for these issues. The question of voting for one or another party is not a matter of public works, it's a broader question. You simply don't have to vote because the government put in water, put in lighting, or resolved the problem of *valas negras* (sewage ditches), and isn't prepared to resolve the problem of wages, to resolve the problem of education, and to really bring about change.[23]

The neighborhood association's initial difficulty in getting its message across suggested to the leadership that the process of reorganization was likely to be a long one. Returns from elections for representatives to Rio's State Assembly in November 1978 confirm that the events of that and the previous year had had little immediate impact on the way people thought about politics, in that Duque captured 37 percent of all votes for MDB candidates for state deputy in the favela.[24] The other big winner, however, was Délio dos Santos, a politician who, like Duque, was affiliated with the MDB but who was not associated with the leadership of Governor Chagas Freitas.[25] Dos Santos was one of a handful of local politicians that had intervened on the favela's behalf in its hour of need, and by way of a reward, he received 35 percent of all votes for MDB candidates for federal deputy in Vidigal. Dos Santos's success in Vidigal was important in that he made significant inroads into the block of votes formerly commanded by the Chaguistas, a block that was now smaller than in many other favelas in Zona Sul.[26]

Furthermore, both the local population's concern over the neighborhood association's decision to sever its contacts with Duque and its fear that this decision would make things more difficult for the favela were soon proven unfounded. As time wore on, the neighborhood association became increasingly adept at organizing support for its efforts and at forcing its way into the offices of the various municipal, state, and federal bureaucracies. Whether by stopping the flow of traffic along the road at the foot of the hill or by camping out in the corridors of the SMDS, the leadership of the neighborhood association quickly established a reputation as a group that could not easily be bought or silenced. More important than its reputation, however, was its success in persuading the state to initiate a series of public works projects in the favela.

In the years immediately following the reactivation of the neighborhood association the favela of Vidigal benefited from, among other things, the construction of a post office, a medical center, and a meeting place for the neighborhood association, the installation of public lighting, the dredging and setting in concrete of some of the largest sewage and drainage ditches on the hill, the installation of a rudimentary water supply system, and the construction of concrete garbage receptacles. Many of these projects were designed, built, and paid for by the neighborhood association itself through the organization of mutirões. The others were financed by donations from the favela's many friends and followers or were part of public works projects initiated by the local state.

In fact, it is interesting and somewhat ironic to note that while the leaders of the neighborhood association are, to a person, highly critical of the politicians that were associated with Chagas Freitas in the

Partido Popular (PP) and, after 1979, in the PMDB, they have nothing but praise for the Chagas Freitas administration itself. By their way of thinking, the Chagas Freitas administration will be remembered not for the politicians that looked to profit from the government's control of public finances but for the creation of the SMDS, the first state agency to develop universal entitlement programs in the favelas and the first to ensure public access to the state. From what we know of the SMDS and of the conflicts that led to the dismisal of Israel Klabin in 1980, it is obvious that the relationship of the leadership of Vidigal with the PMDB was, to a certain extent, a function of its ability to hold the administration to its word.

This does not mean that the Chagas Freitas administration made no attempt to co-opt the neighborhood association in Vidigal. As one of Rio's more organized and, therefore, outspoken favelas, Vidigal benefited from a disproportionate share of the few programs that were developed for such areas. It is clear that the attention that was lavished on Vidigal reflected both the strength of the neighborhood association and the price that the PMDB was willing to pay for its support.

A good illustration of the tension between the PMDB and the neighborhood association in Vidigal is provided by the events surrounding the visit of Pope John Paul II to the favela in June 1980. The announcement of the Pope's visit to Rio and of his intention to spend time in Vidigal prompted the Chagas Freitas administration to initiate a series of public works projects in the favela. Roads were cleaned, drainage ditches dug, and electricity installed in and around the small area of the favela where the Pope was to be led. Chagas Freitas also declared that the ground upon which the favela stood was to be appropriated in the name of "social interest," the first stage in a process that would see the inhabitants of Vidigal in legal possession of their own land.[27]

It was clear to the leadership of the neighborhood association that the governor's declaration of intent to resolve the land tenure issue in Vidigal marked an attempt to convince the Pope; the local, national, and international press; and, to a certain extent, the population of Vidigal that the administration was genuinely concerned with the plight of the urban poor. Not believing for one minute that the administration was about to hand over the deeds to the favela's land, the neighborhood association did its best over the weeks prior to the Pope's arrival to disseminate the idea that both the Pope's visit and the recent improvements to the physical infrastructure of the favela were the result of the community's own efforts and not of political benevolence.[28]

Vidigal and the PDT

Of course, the era of Chaguismo came to somewhat of an abrupt end with the election of Brizola as governor of the state of Rio de Janeiro in November 1982. By all accounts, Brizola and the PDT did exceptionally well in Vidigal, as they did in most favelas of the region. Brizola's victory did little to change the way the neighborhood association went about its business, however. In fact, if anything, the neighborhood association doubled its efforts and increased its demands on an administration that, during the recent election campaign, had declared itself in favor of urbanizing the favelas in Rio.

The neighborhood association's efforts to persuade the Brizola administration to initiate public works projects in Vidigal did not go unrewarded. Over the course of the PDT's first term of office between 1983 and 1987, the administration and the neighborhood association oversaw the completion of the water supply system that had been initiated by the PMDB; the installation of a fairly comprehensive, but still rudimentary, piped sewage system; the long-awaited reform of the public high school at the foot of the hill that because of overenrollment had been forced to run as many as four sittings per day; the construction of Vidigal's own Centro Integrado de Educação Pública (CIEP)–style school; and the resumption of the land appropriation process that, as the neighborhood association had predicted, had stalled soon after the Pope's visit to the favela in 1980.

Brizola's victory in 1982 brought more than its fair share of problems, however. The most serious and potentially damaging of these was associated with the personal appeal of the governor himself. According to the leadership of the neighborhood association, a significant number of those who voted for Brizola in 1982 thought of him as a savior who would resolve all of their problems. Brizola's election, therefore, made it more difficult to persuade people to participate in the neighborhood association, more difficult for the neighborhood association to criticize the PDT's programs, and more difficult for the leadership to convince people that the neighborhood association and not the state was responsible for improvements to the physical and social infrastructure of the favela.

The leadership of the neighborhood association was from the very beginning, therefore, wary of the impact of Brizola's election on favela politics in Rio. Unlike the president of the neighborhood association in Vila Brasil, however, the concern of the leadership of Vidigal was not born solely of the desire to secure a larger slice of the public pie. On the contrary, its concern was, and still is, born of the fear that the leadership of the favela movement in Rio and, by implication, its followers would fail to recognize the similarities between the clientelism of the PMDB and the populism of the PDT.

Part of the problem concerning the relationship between the neighborhood association in Vidigal and the PDT had to do with the politicians that were elected to office in 1982 and with the personnel that were subsequently chosen to administer the agencies in charge of public works in the favelas. The vast majority of those who had worked with neighborhood associations during the era of Chagas Freitas had been members of the so-called independent Left within the PMDB. Brizola's emergence as *the* candidate of the Left in Rio and the restrictions imposed by the voto vinculado meant that not one of these politicians was returned to office in 1982. As a consequence, the vast majority of the PDT's elected officials and its political appointees knew nothing of the history of favela politics in Rio and even less about the organization of public works projects in such areas. Initially, therefore, the leaders of the neighborhood association in Vidigal found themselves being lectured to about issues they had already at least partially resolved.[29]

The dearth of well-known or experienced politicians within the PDT also made it easier for Brizola to exercise a vicelike grip over party policy, a turn of events that created a series of related problems for the neighborhood association in Vidigal. The vast majority of the directors of the neighborhood association in Vidigal are, and since the early 1980s always have been, card-carrying members of the PDT. They are not, however, what you might call typical Brizolistas, in that they are often critical of the party's programs and are more than willing to entertain ideas and suggestions from other political camps.[30] As such, they often find themselves at odds with politicians and functionaries from the PDT who pressure them into toeing the party line. The president of the neighborhood association recalled a recent conversation with a politician from the PDT: "A politician from the PDT told me the other day that Brizola won't tolerate debate. I told him that it's not Brizola's fault, the fault lies with those around him who lack personality. Brizola is only a dictator if you let him be one."[31] Whether one can believe this statement or not is unimportant. What is important is the fact that the neighborhood association in Vidigal is willing to stand up to the PDT despite the fact that it is generally supportive of the party's policies.

The second aspect of the problem concerning the relationship between the neighborhood association in Vidigal and the PDT has to do with pockets of local resistance to the leadership's methods. Despite its many successes over the years and its many attempts to restructure the relationship between the favela and political elites, there are still those who expect the neighborhood association to solicit favors from politicians. The president of the neighborhood association told me:

> Today, there are still people who don't know, who think that it depends on the support of a politician to get anything done. This is very common. People come up to you and say, "Look, I'm after work; don't you know any politician who could help out?" You have to reply, "Wait a minute, if you keep doing this all your life you'll always be stuck on this treadmill." You have to fight to change this. We don't need a savior, nor even a father. I am totally against this paternalism thing, *do tadinho de pobresinho* (pitiful poor little thing). . . . People think that it's good to be *coitadinho* (pitiful) to be able to get favors, I think that these favors are *migalhas* (scraps). When everyone wakes up to the fact that you don't need to ask for favors but have to demand your rights, it's then that I think we'll be able to change things.[32]

Political Competition in Vidigal

Thus far, I have been talking about the neighborhood association as if it were monolithic and as if it were somehow immune to attempts to purchase its favor. Both are fairly accurate statements, however. There has been a remarkable degree of continuity in terms of the personnel that has administered the neighborhood association since it was reinstated in 1978.[33] And the fact that, at any one time, more than twenty people are actively involved in running the favela has meant that those who have controlled the neighborhood association since 1978 have had ample opportunity to cultivate a new generation of leaders with the necessary political experience. Therefore, while a number of the original leaders of the neighborhood association have served at least two terms as president, there is no shortage of candidates to take their place.

The neighborhood association's success in improving the social and physical infrastructure of the favela over the past ten years or so has also meant that its authority is rarely challenged. The current leadership has contested and won seven successive elections for control of the neighborhood association without ever coming close to losing. Therefore, if there are those who disagree with the way that the neighborhood association goes about its business, they are very much in the minority.

The cohesiveness and the prestige of the neighborhood association in Vidigal have, in turn, made it easier for the leadership to resist the temptation to use its power to its own or someone else's advantage. I say easier, because the directors of the neighborhood association are under fairly constant pressure to favor one party or faction over another. This pressure stems from two sources: personal political loyalties and sources of individual livelihood.

As already mentioned, the vast majority of the directors of the neighborhood association are open supporters of the PDT. Many, however, identify with other political parties, in particular with the Partido dos Trabalhadores (PT), the PMDB, the PFL, and the Partido da Social Democracia Brasileiro (PSDB). This means that debates among the directors of the neighborhood association often mirror those of larger political society. Not only do the directors of the neighborhood association identify with different political parties, many are also employed by these

A typical alleyway in Vidigal

A view of Avenida João Goulart with Ipanema visible in the distance

A view of Vidigal facing southeast

One of the few wooden constructions remaining in Vidigal

Vidigal's cultural center

An example of "urbanized" sewage collection

A typical drainage and sewage ditch in Vidigal

The principal drainage and sewage ditch as it leaves Vidigal for the ocean

same parties in some capacity or other.[34] In most cases, offers of employment are accompanied by demands for political fealty. Those who find themselves in this position do their best to keep such things from their mind while fulfilling their obligations as directors of the neighborhood association. Those among the directors who are not associated with the PDT complain, however, that they are often outnumbered and outmaneuvered.[35]

Of course, the neighborhood association is also by no means the only organization of any influence in Vidigal. The favela is home to a large number of churches of different denominations, a large and extremely active samba block, and a soccer club. Each of these organizations plays a role in the social and political life of the favela, some more than others. Until fairly recently, however, most of these organizations complemented and even assisted the work of the neighborhood association in Vidigal.[36]

In recent years, however, the neighborhood association has had to contend with the increasingly powerful and intrusive presence of *traficantes* (drug dealers) in the favela. In years past, the drug gang enjoyed a relatively good relationship with the population of Vidigal in that for the most part it kept out of the day-to-day affairs of the favela. During the past four or five years, however, the drug gang has become increasingly violent in its dealings with other traficantes, with the local police, and with residents of the favela itself. At the same time, however, the drug gang has been cultivating its own basis of support in the favela by financing small public works projects at the top of the slum and by making the occasional donation of a truckload of food and provisions to the more needy families of the community.

At any one time, the drug gang in Vidigal consists of thirty or so men in their late teens or early twenties who are recruited from the ranks of the favela population. The gang owns a considerable number of houses, or *bocas de fumo*, in different parts of the favela, and from these it sells marijuana and cocaine. The bocas de fumo and all points of entry to the favela are closely watched and heavily guarded, a precautionary measure in the event of a raid by the local police. More often than not, however, intrusions by the police fail in their attempts to apprehend gang members. They fail because of the inaccessibility of much of the favela, because the drug traffickers have been alerted beforehand by police in their pay, or because what the police are really after is a larger share of the profits.

The life expectancy of those who sell drugs in Vidigal is extremely short.[37] There is never a shortage of volunteers, however. Apart from a free supply of cocaine and marijuana, a share in the considerable profits to be made from the sale of drugs in Vidigal is incentive enough when compared with the humiliation, drudgery, long hours, and low pay associated with jobs open to favelados in the city.[38]

The increasingly powerful presence of the drug gang is a source of some concern to the leadership of Vidigal, not so much because of increasing levels of violence, but because the traficantes are, in a sense, competing with the neighborhood association for the hearts and minds of the local population. The neighborhood association has nothing like the financial resources of the drug gang so it has been forced to redouble its efforts to improve the quality of services in the favela.

This situation has become more difficult because Brazil's economy has been mired in a deep recession since the early 1980s. The recession has meant that many more young men in Vidigal now consider selling drugs for a living.[39] It has also meant that government funding for public works projects in the favelas has been in even shorter supply. On the other hand, however, the recession has meant that many families and individuals in Vidigal are now even more dependent on the services and assistance offered by the neighborhood association, so there has been no noticeable decline in levels of popular participation or in the general standing of the neighborhood association itself. It is fairly safe to say, therefore, that as long as the neighborhood association continues to be successful in its efforts to represent the favela's interests its position is unlikely to be challenged. If for whatever reason, however, conditions in the favela deteriorate, then the neighborhood association might well have a battle on its hands.

Conclusion

If fifteen years ago you had stumbled across the favela of Vidigal, you would have encountered a settlement much like any number of others in Rio de Janeiro. It would have consisted of a haphazard collection of simple, makeshift wooden shacks. Inside these shacks you would have found the working poor, surviving at the very margins of existence. On closer inspection you also would have found a community that was socially isolated and politically disorganized, its welfare in the hands of a local political broker whose concern for the population of the favela manifested itself during brief periods of electoral activity.

Vidigal is still, by anyone's definition, a favela. It is, however, a very different favela. The past ten years or so have witnessed a dramatic trans-formation in the physical structure of the place. During this time the process of urbanization has turned Vidigal into a permanent feature of the city landscape. This change has not just been physical, however. The favela has undergone an equally dramatic political transformation. The neighborhood association, once a last-ditch vehicle of popular resistance to removal, now commands a permanent and unrivaled position in the favela. Furthermore, the leadership of the neighborhood association has effectively withdrawn from politics as it used to be conducted in Vidigal by redefining its relationship with political and administrative elites and by refusing to exchange votes for favors.

This means that instead of soliciting the support of politicians who promise to intervene on the favela's behalf, the neighborhood asso-ciation now takes its demands directly to the various municipal, state, and federal government offices downtown. More important, however, it means that the population of Vidigal is no longer dependent on such politicians or mechanisms of political representation to get things done in the favela, thus challenging the very basis of clientelist and populist politics.

The catalyst for this transformation was the ill-fated attempt to re-move the favela from its present site in 1977. This single event brought the favela into contact with a comprehensive network of popular orga-nizations and popular representatives intent on redefining the rules of the political game by challenging the arbitrariness of authoritarian rule.

It also exposed the leadership of Vidigal to new conceptions of citizenship and very different forms of political participation and organization. And if the conditions that sparked waves of popular protest against the military regime in the late 1970s and early 1980s no longer exist, the legacy of the transition period is still very much in evidence in the favela of Vidigal.

4

THE COMING OF ELECTIONS

The neighborhood associations that we encountered in the favelas of Vila Brasil and Vidigal represent common yet contrasting responses to urban poverty in Rio. The neighborhood association in Vila Brasil, on the one hand, has evolved in ways that reflect its president's efforts to make the most of the limited opportunities provided by clientelist politics. The neighborhood association in Vidigal, on the other hand, has evolved in ways that reflect its leadership's steadfast refusal to exchange votes for favors. Nowhere were the differences between the two favelas more marked than in the events leading up to the elections in Rio in November 1986.

Election Politics in Vila Brasil

THE BARGAIN
The prospect of elections for a new governor, two new senators, forty-six federal deputies, and seventy state deputies in November 1986 was eagerly awaited by the president of the neighborhood association in Vila

Brasil. For while the president enjoyed a degree of success in his efforts to improve the quality of life in the favela at different times throughout his term of office, it was during elections that he achieved his most notable successes. His reputation as president of the neighborhood association had, after all, been established on the basis of his ability to turn out the vote. The vote was, therefore, by far the most powerful weapon in his arsenal. Because in 1986 there were twenty-eight different political parties competing for a relatively small number of offices, the president expected that, come late August or early September, the neighborhood association would be besieged by candidates.

By July, the president had already determined the favela's asking price for that year. Initially, he toyed with the idea of persuading a candidate to pay for the installation of a legal water supply. The community's water was, at the time of the elections, supplied through an illegal hookup to the official system that served the surrounding area. On further reflection, however, the president decided that it was not such a good idea after all, since the favela's current water supply worked reasonably well and was free of charge. Instead, he set his sights on three smaller yet no less significant projects.

The first of these was to persuade a candidate to pay for the construction of a second story on top of the neighborhood association building. The expansion of the neighborhood association building was something the president had been working on for a long time but had never been able to finish. The second project was to get someone to pay for the installation of two new bathrooms in the recreational area at the back of the neighborhood association building. The third was to persuade candidates to donate building materials so that the president could continue his efforts to convert all houses in Vila Brasil from wood to brick.[1]

By the beginning of August, the president of the neighborhood association was on the receiving end of at least one phone call a day from candidates who were looking to buy the community's vote. Most of these candidates were simply feeling the president out, however, and were as yet unprepared to put any money up front. In fact, as time wore on, the president became increasingly concerned that no one would be willing to meet his asking price. He attributed the lack of interest in the favela to the fact that the Tribunal Superior Eleitoral (the governing electoral administration) was taking an inordinate amount of time to define the rules governing alliances between the different political parties in Rio, which in turn determined the distribution of candidacies. It was only in mid September, when the rules governing interparty alliances were clarified and when campaign publicity hit the television screens that the president was able to start bargaining in earnest.

Nonetheless, by the end of August the president had received five firm offers to pay for the construction of the second story of the neighborhood association building. These offers were made by candidates for federal and state deputy for the Partido da Frente Liberal (PFL), the Partido do Movimento Democrático Brasileiro (PMDB), the Partido Democrático Trabalhista (PDT), the Partido Democrático Cristão (PDC), and the Partido Socialista Agrário e Renovador Trabalhista (PASART). The president told each candidate that the first one to come up with the necessary money to begin work on the project could be assured of the community's vote. Of the initial five, the PASART candidate for state deputy, Noé Martins, appeared the most interested. On August 20, Martins drove up to the neighborhood association building with his team of campaign advisors to inform the president that he was willing to pay for the materials and the labor necessary to complete the project. A local evangelical priest, Martins talked briefly about his political credentials and about his ideas for the future if elected to Rio's State Assembly, then began thrashing out the details of the bargain. The president's side of the bargain was to campaign for Martins in Vila Brasil and to draw up a list of all the names and addresses of the neighborhood association's three hundred or so members. This list was then to be turned over to Martins so that the candidate could use it to distribute his campaign publicity.

As agreed, the president compiled a list of names and addresses of all the members of the neighborhood association in Vila Brasil. Well versed in the various tricks of his trade, however, he refused to hand over the list until Martins came up with the money to cover the cost of the construction project and to pay for the secretary of the neighborhood association and a friend to distribute the candidate's campaign literature. In his days as a cabo eleitoral for Jorge Leite, the president of Vila Brasil had been tricked into paying for the distribution of campaign publicity from his own pocket. He was not, therefore, about to make the same mistake. The president was also well aware that once he handed over the list of names and addresses, Martins would in all likelihood bypass the neighborhood association and canvass its members directly. Sure enough, within a week of the president making these demands it was obvious that Martins had lost much of his initial interest. The president subsequently locked the list of names and addresses in the neighborhood association's safe and called off the deal.

During this time, the president of Vila Brasil received innumerous telephone calls from Ubaldo de Oliveira, a former state deputy and ex-Chaguista who was now running for office for the PDT.[2] Oliveira was calling to tell the president to forget about Martins and to come work for him in his bid for reelection. He received similar phone calls from Jorge Leite (PMDB candidate for federal deputy) and Renato Vasconcellos (PFL candidate for state deputy), both of whom he had worked for in the past. Leite and Vasconcellos attempted to convince the president that he owed them for past services rendered. In the absence of any guarantees of future material gain, however, the president was unwilling to make any sort of commitment to either one. In fact, he told Leite that if politicians could change parties so readily, he did not see why he shouldn't either.

By mid September, the president of Vila Brasil had given up hope of persuading anyone to pay for the construction of the second story of the neighborhood association building. He figured that either the asking price was too high or that the votes he was promising to deliver were perceived to be too few. This seemed strange at the time, since with so many candidates running for office, the number of votes necessary for election was considerably less than at any time in the past. If the president was beginning to despair of anyone paying for the second story of the neighborhood association, he had, nonetheless, received offers of a different kind from two PMDB candidates for state deputy. Carlos Alberto Rodrigues had already donated the customary set of shirts to the favela's soccer club and was promising to hand over another if the president assisted him in his campaign. Henrique Oswaldo, on the other hand, had offered to pay for the construction of the two bathrooms at the back of the neighborhood association building. Not surprisingly, the president of Vila Brasil devoted most of his time and energy to Oswaldo.

President of a tourist company, engineer, professor, and sometime advisor to Leonel Brizola's administration, Oswaldo was a relative newcomer to politics and a very different breed of political animal than Leite and his ex-Chaguista associates within the PMDB. Oswaldo's campaign platform was to give voice to the interests of the tourist industry in Rio. Needless to say, this was of little immediate interest to the population of Vila Brasil. Oswaldo's appeal in Vila Brasil was, therefore, based on a very different kind of political platform. It was based purely and simply on his writing a check to pay for the materials and labor necessary for the construction of two bathrooms at the back of the neighborhood association building. Thus, if Oswaldo was not a Chaguista he was, nonetheless, extremely interested in the idea of a cheap and readily available source of votes.

Over the course of the next six weeks, the president of the neighborhood association and Oswaldo engaged in a long and drawn out sparring match, with each trying his best to turn the final deal to his maximum advantage. Oswaldo instructed the president to estimate how much the construction of the two bathrooms would cost. The president obliged and came up with the figure of 11,000 cruzeiros (roughly $800 at the time). Oswaldo then protested that the cost of the project was too high for the number of votes that the president was promising to deliver and threatened to pull out of the deal.[3] Wary of the possibility that the deal might fall through, the president went ahead with the distribution of the candidate's campaign literature and the erection of a few posters. Without the promised cash in hand, however, he was as yet unwilling to introduce Oswaldo to the favela as "his" candidate.

During this time, the president would make almost daily telephone calls to Oswaldo's office in downtown Rio. In his conversations he would tell Oswaldo that everyone in the favela was pressing him for information about whom they should vote for in the forthcoming elections, thereby creating the impression that the entire favela was at his beck and call. Then the president would tell Oswaldo how unfortunate it was that he was not yet able to advertise the candidate's name since Oswaldo had not yet come up with the money. Occasionally, the president's conversations prompted Oswaldo to set a time and date when he would appear in the favela. Deadlines of when the money would be handed over were subsequently agreed upon and then broken. At more than one point in the proceedings it looked as though the deal would fall through.

Finally, just ten days before the day of the election, Oswaldo appeared at the neighborhood association with a check for the two bathrooms. He was then escorted through the favela from door to door and presented as "the president's candidate." The president explained to the inhabitants of each household that Oswaldo had just handed him a check for the construction of two new bathrooms at the back of the neighborhood association building and that, having done so, he more than deserved their support on November 15.

Oswaldo's initial introduction to the population of Vila Brasil was only the first stage in the campaign process, however. In the days that remained prior to the election the president paid the neighborhood association's secretary and a friend to distribute Oswaldo's campaign literature to every household in the favela and, although strictly illegal, to canvass voters on the candidate's behalf at local polling stations on election day.

THE ESSENCE OF CLIENTELIST POLITICS

The contract between the president of the neighborhood association in Vila Brasil and Oswaldo provides a perfect illustration of both the form and the logic of contemporary clientelist politics in Rio. The president of the neighborhood association had learned from past experience never to campaign for a candidate without first receiving the money up front. He thus guaranteed that both the neighborhood association and the candidate stood to gain from the bargain. So adamant was he on this point that he would have rather forgone the opportunity to make money than to have sold the vote for less than he thought it was worth.

The president of the neighborhood association also had little contact with Oswaldo either before or after the election. In fact, the president knew nothing of Oswaldo until the two first spoke with each other on the telephone. While the president was to have many subsequent conversations with Oswaldo, he met the candidate in person on only a couple of occasions. After the election was over, the only time the two men spoke was when Oswaldo called to complain that he had received very few votes in the area. As it turned out, Oswaldo's bid for a seat in the State Assembly proved unsuccessful. Even if Oswaldo had been elected, however, he would have been under no obligation to attend to the requests of the president of Vila Brasil. The deal was, for all intents and purposes, over and done with.

The fact that the president of the neighborhood association reached an agreement with a candidate from the PMDB in 1982 and 1986 might create the impression that, despite protests to the contrary, the president of Vila Brasil felt obliged to continue working for a party that had served him well in the past. Nothing could be further from the truth, however. In fact, if anything, the PMDB was rapidly becoming the president's least favorite of all of the political parties in Rio.

The president of Vila Brasil's decision to support Leite in 1982 and Oswaldo in 1986 was dictated purely and simply by their willingness to pay a better price than other candidates in the field. It just so happened that the two men were affiliated with the same political party.[4] And the fact that the president of the neighborhood association shook on a deal with Oswaldo ten days before the election did nothing to discourage him from talking to candidates from other parties. In fact, in 1986 the president ended up working, in some capacity or another for four candidates without any one of them finding out about the existence of the other three![5]

If the president of the neighborhood association felt any loyalty toward a political party it was, increasingly, toward the PDT. Since Brizola's victory in 1982, the PDT had been paying considerable attention to the favelas of Zona Oeste and tempting the president with the kind of fringe benefits he had once received from the PMDB. The president was both impressed by the PDT's work in the region and flattered by the party's respect for him as a local political broker. He was not yet willing, however, to throw in his lot with the PDT. Nor was he prepared to forego the opportunites provided by a major election.

The one candidate for the PDT to gain the president of Vila Brasil's respect, to the point where he even considered working for him, was Carlos Alberto de Oliveira, popularly known as Caó. Caó was at the time state secretary of housing and labor and had been responsible for overseeing the administration's efforts to legalize the tenure of a number of favelas in Zona Oeste. The president of the neighborhood association approved of this program and hoped that some day soon it would be extended to the favela of Vila Brasil.

One month prior to the election, however, Caó attempted to turn a regional Federação da Associações de Favelas do Estado do Rio de Janeiro (FAFERJ) congress that was organized to discuss the issue of land tenure into a rally in support of his bid for a seat in the Federal House of Representatives. Frustrated by the resistance of the leadership of FAFERJ in Zona Oeste to the PDT's overtures, Caó proceeded to admonish those present for their reluctance in pledging their support in spite of all that the administration had done in the area.[6]

The regional executive of FAFERJ was incensed by Caó's outburst and by his attempt to blackmail the leadership of the favelas into voting for the PDT. The president of Vila Brasil was also incensed—not, however, because the PDT had revealed that it was in the business of buying votes but because the party was attempting to undermine the autonomy of the local favela leadership.[7] Unlike the leadership of FAFERJ in Zona Oeste, the president of Vila Brasil saw nothing wrong in voting for politicians who were willing to make good on their promises. This was, after all, the essence of clientelist politics. What upset the president of Vila Brasil was the fact that the PDT wanted him to give up his right to decide whom he and his many followers should support. Past experience had taught the president that his ability to take advantage of elections was based on his willingness to make a deal with the highest bidder and his ability to play one politician or party off against another. Somewhat ironically, therefore, the president of Vila Brasil was as determined as the regional executive of FAFERJ to defend the principle of political autonomy and was as much, if not more, of an obstacle to the PDT's success in the region.

THE POPULAR BASIS OF CLIENTELISM

The president of Vila Brasil's reputation as a political broker rests more than anything on his ability to turn out the vote. The extent to which he is able to take advantage of elections depends, therefore, on the complicity of the population of Vila Brasil. The complicity of the population of Vila Brasil rests, in turn, on the president's continued success as a political broker. There is, therefore, a built-in incentive for the president of the neighborhood association to pursue better and ever more productive deals. As long as the president continues to enjoy success in his negotiations with politicians and administrators, there will always be those who are more than willing to abide by his decisions.

It would be wrong to suggest, however, that the neighborhood association is the only influence on political behavior in Vila Brasil. In 1986, for example, the since-defunct samba block, G.R.B.C. Boca na Garrafa, distributed its own campaign literature in the favela, displaying its lyric for the next year's carnival and the names of three candidates that had donated money to the organization.[8] The samba block, though important, had less say over how people voted than the neighborhood association did, however.

It would also be wrong to suggest that everyone in Vila Brasil identifies with the president of the neighborhood association and that everyone assists the neighborhood association in its efforts to improve the favela. The president chooses not to discriminate against those who do not subscribe to the neighborhood association, and there will certainly be those who take advantage of this situation. It should be remembered, however, that as the inhabitants of a favela, the population of Vila Brasil faces a common set of difficult circumstances that tends, in itself, to favor collective courses of action.[9]

Finally, as we saw in the case of the elections in 1986, it is rare for the president of Vila Brasil to use his influence to promote more than one candidate at any one time. Therefore, while the president of the neighborhood association is open to the idea of accepting money from as many candidates as possible, he spends time campaigning only for those who are willing to make a substantial financial investment in the favela. This means that in any given election, the population of Vila Brasil is "free" to vote for whomever it pleases at all but one or, on the rare occasion, two levels of the dispute.

The candidates that the president of the neighborhood association tends to work with are, almost without exception, those that run for a seat on the City Council, in Rio's State Assembly, or in the Federal House of Representatives. There are basically three reasons for this. First, candidates for city councilman, state deputy, and federal deputy are less likely to be known outside of their immediate political constituencies and are less likely to enjoy access to the media and other political forums than are candidates for higher public office. This means that they tend to rely far more heavily on the cultivation of local bases of support and on the type of face-to-face contact that clientelist politics provides. Second, because candidates for city councilman, state deputy, and federal deputy often lack name recognition and access to the media, voters are often themselves less informed when it comes to making choices at lower levels of the election, meaning that they too are more dependent on the type of information that clientelism provides.

Finally, that the absolute number of positions to be filled on the City Council, in the State Assembly, and in the Federal House of Representatives is far greater than in the Senate or in the governor's palace means that candidates for the lower positions of public office need far fewer votes to be elected. The construction of a political constituency on the basis of clientelism is, therefore, a far more attractive and viable proposition for candidates for lower than for higher levels of public office.

This is not to say that clientelism, in the manner that it is practiced in Vila Brasil, plays no part in the election of senators, governors, or even presidents in Rio. After all, the political power of Antônio de Pádua Chagas Freitas during the late 1960s and throughout the 1970s was based on his command of a network of personal fiefdoms of precisely the kind articulated by Leite in Vila Brasil. It should be remembered, however, that the power of the Chaguistas in Rio owed much to the fact that the Movimento Democrático Brasileiro (MDB) was, to a large extent, the only game in town and that their collective, if not individual, demise was in no small part a product of political liberalization.

The fact that the president of the neighborhood association rarely promotes more than one candidate for political office in any given election does not mean, however, that he has no influence on how people vote at other levels of the dispute. The president's success over the past ten years or so has taught a generation of voters in Vila Brasil to support candidates that make good on their promises and to steer clear of those who do not. This much was clear to me during my many conversations with the president and with the residents of the favela.

As election day drew near the president would be stopped on his rounds wherever he went in the favela and asked by people of all ages who it was that the neighborhood association was working with that year. On occasions, the conversation would be limited to those candidates who had offered the president money. More often than not, however, the conversation extended to other candidates that the president thought worthwhile supporting for one reason or another.

As I was interested in the strength and nature of the president's support in Vila Brasil, I asked him to introduce me to those individuals and families most closely associated with his leadership. The ensuing conversations, of which the following is but a sample, illustrate clearly how the president has used his office and his considerable political acumen to build a large and loyal following in the favela. Each of the interviewees was asked to describe conditions in the favela before the president took office and to explain how the physical transformation of the favela came about. They were also asked if they themselves followed the president's advice with regard to political candidates. One man in his seventies responded to my questions in the following manner:

> I've lived here for twenty years. There's no comparing what it was like then and what it's like now. It was a pile of mud, alleys full of rubbish, without lighting, without piped water. . . . There were bandits around that have since disappeared; it's much better. It improved because of the efforts of our president.

When asked if he supports candidates that the president recommends, he replied:

> Yes, I support him. . . . Anyone who's done something here has got our vote. Whoever the president says, we're with him.[10]

A second interviewee described the president's record thus:

> The first time I arrived here, back home from work, I felt like putting all my things on my back and leaving again. Because when it rained hard at night you used to have to walk around with water

up to your knees. I was already tired, but I felt like I was going to die. Then things got better and better, I got to know senhor Boar, who, by then, was president. Lighting came, paving came, everything came. I don't consider this a favela. . . . It was Boar who negotiated for us. Where these things came from I don't know; I know that it was him that did these things. I believe in him, everything that he says happens. Seventy percent of the favela vote for the candidate he asks for.[11]

A woman in her mid forties with nine children described her relationship with the president:

The paving was his doing; after he took over the presidency he had all the roads paved, even this alleyway here, after he was made president. The president brought sewage, paving, water, lighting, improvements in the houses that were falling to pieces. He helped us, he asked for things . . . and it was done, all of this. If he asks, I vote. I think that what needed to be done has already been done here. He's always looking to improve things even more. Here, in this house, there are plenty of people who vote. There are ten voters here, me and my nine children. My husband, he votes however he wishes. We here, who depend on the community, vote for whoever has brought us benefits or for the candidate that Boar thinks is good for us here.[12]

And, finally, a man in his forties confirmed what the others had said before:

I don't think there can be a better favela than this one. At least when I arrived here, the place was full of mud. All there were, were marginals, which today there aren't any longer. . . . Everyone he brings here we support because we are well satisfied with his administration in this area.[13]

Election Politics in Vidigal

BUSINESS AS USUAL

The November 15, 1986, elections were as important to the leadership of Vidigal as they were to the president of Vila Brasil, but for very different reasons. They were important not because they provided an opportunity to get things done in the favela but because they represented a referendum on competing visions of social and economic justice—one of those rare occasions when the general public has a say in the distribution of political power in society. Unlike the neighborhood association in Vila Brasil, however, the neighborhood association in Vidigal took no active part in the proceedings.

There was little or no change in the routine of the neighborhood association in Vidigal during the three months in which the elections commanded the attention of the local and national press. The neighborhood association continued to meet on a weekly basis and to concern itself with the day-to-day administration of the favela. The neighborhood association also continued to pressure the state to honor its various promises and commitments, despite the fact that almost all of the local government offices were themselves gearing up for the forthcoming contest. This does not mean that the leaders of the neighborhood association expressed no interest in the outcome of the election. It meant, however, that the leaders of Vidigal expressed no interest in the election in their capacities as representatives of the neighborhood association.

The leadership of Vidigal was fully aware that many neighborhood associations in Rio offer their services to candidates prior to elections and that their willingness to vote for the highest bidder can often produce spectacular results. The leadership of Vidigal refused to be party to this kind of deal, however, arguing that the exchange of votes for favors constitutes an abuse of the neighborhood association's power and a strategy that is detrimental to the favela population's long-term interests. The leadership of Vidigal firmly believed, therefore, that if the neighborhood association's mandate is to improve conditions in the favela, it should not have to do this by telling people how to vote. One of the directors of the neighborhood association explained his feelings toward this issue:

> There are many neighborhood associations that are tied to a certain party. . . . We know there are many associations that work like that, that are linked not even to a party but to a politician and persuade the community to support that person. Like this you don't give people the liberty to think for themselves. People have to think and to vote wrong if necessary. The Brazilian people have to be able to vote for whom they want; not everyone thinks alike. Therefore, you can't control the neighborhood association or use it for political purposes, determining that everyone should vote for a certain person, no. You have to give people the liberty to vote for good candidates and bad candidates. This is the job that we're doing.[14]

Of course, it is important to remember that the leadership of the neighborhood association in Vidigal was only in a position to be critical of other neighborhood associations because of its relative success in pursuing its more immediate demands through alternative channels and because it was not, and is not, controlled by any one individual, political party, or faction.

The fact that the leadership of Vidigal was openly dismissive of the tactics routinely employed by other neighborhood associations in Rio does not mean, however, that it made no attempt to turn the elections to its own advantage. On the contrary, the directors of the neighborhood association were on the constant lookout for candidates who were willing to help the community in one way or other. Toward the end of one neighborhood association meeting in mid September, the president stood up and asked if anyone in the audience knew of a cabo eleitoral whose candidate was looking to "invest" money in the favela. He then qualified the invitation by making it perfectly clear that no one in Vidigal would be obliged to vote for such an individual.

As it turned out, the neighborhood association received numerous offers from candidates in the months preceding the election. The most significant of these came from none other than Nelson Moreira Franco, the brother of the PMDB's candidate for governor, Wellington Moreira Franco. Nelson Moreira Franco's proposal was to pay for the construction of a third story on top of the neighborhood association building and for the project to be inaugurated by his brother.[15] The directors of the neighborhood association discussed the offer at one of their weekly meetings and decided to accept, on condition that the project include a complete overhaul of the entire neighborhood association building and that Nelson Moreira Franco understand that the leadership was under no obligation to support his brother in the forthcoming election. Needless to say, the offer never materialized.

Then, in October, a PDT candidate for federal deputy telephoned the neighborhood association and offered to pave the upper reaches of Avenida João Goulart. Before the neighborhood association would agree to anything, however, it wanted a guarantee that the job would be done properly. The leadership knew from experience that, in most cases, offers such as these meant that asphalt would be hurriedly laid down on top of the original dirt surface and that, within a year, the road would be in even worse condition than before. Once again, the offer was summarily withdrawn.

In addition to these offers of assistance, the neighborhood association also received a number of small gifts. As a longtime friend of the favela, PFL candidate for state deputy Renato Vasconcellos provided a fleet of buses and held a barbecue for one of the soccer club's outings to a town outside of Rio in October. Alberto Souto, to cite another example, donated the now-customary set of shirts to the soccer club in his capacity as candidate for state deputy for the little known Partido Humanista (PH). Both gifts were accepted with open arms.

POLITICAL DEBATE

If the leadership of Vidigal's neighborhood association refused to use its considerable authority to tell people who they should vote for, it did spend a considerable amount of time and energy in an attempt to influence the way people voted. The leadership went to great lengths to explain why it was a mistake to vote for a politician on the basis of what he or she had done for the favela in the past, and how the problems that confronted Vidigal were problems that confronted the urban poor in general. The leadership was, therefore, less concerned with the relative merits of any one candidate over another than it was with the strengths and weaknesses of each party's political programs. The trick, however, was to convince others of the wisdom of this philosophy.

One way in which the leadership brought the election to the attention of the local population was to invite candidates for office to present their ideas and platforms at the weekly neighborhood association meetings. This meant that there were anywhere from one to five different candidates present on a Wednesday night throughout the final two months of the campaign. At these meetings the directors of the neighborhood association would go about their business in their usual meticulous style, reporting on the most minute details of the past week's events and commenting on their negotiations with the various arms of the local state. Having made the candidates wait for an hour or so, the directors would call on them to introduce themselves and to say something about their future plans, if elected.

Most of the candidates that attended these meetings were running for office for the PMDB, the PDT, or the Partido Socialista Brasileiro (PSB). All were acutely aware of their audience and of the need to say the "right things." Hence, there was much talk of democracy, of the importance of a strong and politically independent favela movement, and of the need for popular participation in government. The meetings were interesting, nonetheless, in that they ended with what was often a heated debate among the candidates and in that they provided those present with a unique opportunity to ask questions about a variety of issues. Most important of all, however, was the fact that the meetings demonstrated that it was possible to talk about politics in a manner that went beyond the issues of bricks and mortar.

Apart from its weekly meetings with the different candidates, the neighborhood association also played an important role in turning people out on election day and in explaining what was a fairly complicated system of voting. This was particularly significant in the context of the elections in 1986 because successful candidates to the Federal House of Representatives and the Senate were to be responsible for drafting a new constitution. And although no one in Vidigal had much of an idea of how the new legislative body would function, at every opportunity the neighborhood association promoted discussion of the implications of constitutional reform.

The level of political debate in Vidigal in the months before the election was greatly enhanced by a congress that was organized by the Pastoral de Favelas of Zona Sul in mid August. The idea behind the congress was to bring together representatives from all of the region's favelas to talk about the present constitution, about why it was not working, and about what should be included in the new one. The participants in the debate exhibited a highly sophisticated grasp of a wide range of issues, including anything from the relative monetary value of manual versus intellectual labor, the death penalty, a realistic minimum wage, the role of women in society, and the problem of police violence.

Not surprisingly, the topic of conversation also turned to the forthcoming elections. Four resolutions were discussed by the hundred or so people present. The first of these was that the favelas should vote only for candidates from the popular classes. The second was that these same candidates should be involved with the popular movement prior to the elections. The third resolution stipulated that these candidates should have no ties with the military, and the fourth that the favela population of Zona Sul should perhaps decide to back one candidate over and above all others.

It was clear from the start that the final resolution was problematic in that few of the leaders that were present felt comfortable with the idea of pushing certain candidates over others. Nevertheless, the fact that the issue came up at all and was seriously considered suggests that it is not beyond the realm of all possibility. The first resolution also proved to be problematic in that candidates from the popular classes tend to be few and far between and that the simple fact of being from the popular classes, let alone from the favelas, is not in itself a necessarily good criterion for voting. The other two resolutions, however, were ones that I had heard mentioned in many other contexts and were certainly ones that the leadership of Vidigal had discussed at length with its own membership. More important than the outcome of the debate, however, was that such an event could be organized in the first place and that everyone present, including the leadership of Vidigal, expressed concern for a series of issues that affected the urban poor as a social class.[16]

POLITICAL PRESSURE

Campaign debates were not, of course, restricted to the confines of the neighborhood association. In the final months prior to the election the favela of Vidigal was besieged by candidates and awash with campaign literature. Hardly a building in the favela was left untouched. And if the various candidates who visited the favela during this time were aware of the fact that Vidigal was not fertile ground for the more traditional forms of electioneering, this did not prevent them from employing alternative tactics.

Of particular importance in this regard was the relationship between the directors of the neighborhood association and the PDT. For example, it was soon clear to the president of the neighborhood association that the PDT fully expected him, as a card-carrying party member, to mobilize support in Vidigal on the basis of the public works projects that the administration had initiated in the favela since taking office in 1983. While generally sympathetic to the party's cause, the president was incensed by the suggestion that he should use his authority as a representative of the neighborhood association to drum up support for the PDT in Vidigal.

The president was incensed because although the PDT had been relatively forthcoming with funds for various projects in the favela, it was by no means the first or the only party to make good on its promises. Second, and most important, the PDT was telling the president and, by implication, the population of Vidigal that it should be grateful for what the neighborhood association had been saying all along were basic rights of citizenship. He explained his dilemma in the following manner: "This guy wanted to convince me that the PDT had made a lot of improvements here in Vidigal. It was really difficult for me to explain to him that it wasn't so. I told him that the PDT hadn't done much here and that I was in the PDT for much broader issues."[17] The neighborhood association also came under considerable pressure from former PDT secretaries who were looking to cash in on the administration's work in the favelas to boost their own political campaigns.[18] The most important of these in terms of the favela of Vidigal were Luis Alfredo Salamão (former state secretary for public works) and Caó (former state secretary of housing and labor). Both Salamão and Caó were PDT candidates for federal deputy in 1986.

Salamão had been the director of the program that had installed piped sewage and water in many favelas in the state, including Vidigal. Salamão asked the president of the neighborhood association in Vidigal if he could visit the favela in his capacity as a candidate for a seat in the

Federal House of Representatives. The president told Salamão that he was more than welcome to campaign in Vidigal on condition that he did not ask for votes on the basis of the work that the PDT had recently initiated in the favela. The president explained to Salamão why it was that the neighborhood association did not want people to associate public works with votes and how, in any case, the sewage and water systems were so badly maintained that they were more of a liability than an asset. The outcome of this conversation was that Salamão decided that his time might be better spent elsewhere.

The relationship between the neighborhood association and Caó was somewhat different. Caó was overseeing the appropriation of the favela's land, a process that had been initiated by Chagas Freitas back in 1980 but that had not yet reached fruition. The neighborhood association was, nonetheless, extremely impressed by Caó's attitude toward his work in the favela. According to the president, Caó was by far the most competent and trustworthy of the secretaries in the Brizola administration *because* he had not used his position as a springboard for his campaign. The leadership of the neighborhood association was, of course, unaware of the events involving Caó and the favela leadership of Zona Oeste. The fact that Caó did not even try to make the connection between what he was doing in Vidigal and his forthcoming candidacy spoke volumes for the reputation of the favela, however.

Further evidence of the neighborhood association's ability to influence its negotiations with the state was provided by the way the issue of land tenure was handled in Vidigal. It is common in Brazil for administrations to initiate public works projects on the eve of major elections. This sudden frenzy of activity is designed to refresh the memory of the loyal voter and to make believers of those who might fear that such projects would not be completed lest the party in office be reelected. Wary of this strategy, the neighborhood association in Vidigal did all it could to resolve the issue of land tenure before the election. The last thing it wanted was to be forced into a position whereby it felt obliged to support the PDT for fear of jeopardizing what, historically, had been one of its most pressing demands.

Predictably, however, the project came to a grinding halt right before the elections. Part of the problem was bureaucratic, associated with the complexities of land appropriation and compensation. To be fair to the PDT, however, the other part of the problem had to do with the difficulties of sorting out competing claims to land among the population of Vidigal itself.[19] Either way, there was little that the leadership could do about the matter so close to an election. Rather than rushing it through to satisfy the political interests of the PDT, the directors of the neighborhood association decided to abandon the project altogether. The president explained the thinking behind the leadership of the neighborhood association's decision:

> After the election we are really going to have to come down hard on the public agencies and government secretaries so that these projects are executed independently of who wins or loses. I don't even want to know. I know that we are going to have to fight and that these projects have to be carried through, and without these guys coming here to blackmail us, saying that they'll do the work but we have to vote for them. I reckon that as long as we are here in control of the neighborhood association, we're never going to allow this.[20]

As idealistic and naive as this might sound, the unanimity and resolve of the neighborhood association in Vidigal was effective in disarming attempts to bully the leadership into entering the political fray. This does not mean that public works projects do not generate votes in Vidigal but rather that the neighborhood association's success in getting things done without selling itself to the highest bidder means that there is no obvious connection between the two.

Because the leadership of the neighborhood association is so wary of the more crude attempts to buy votes in the favela, the campaign in Vidigal operated at a far more sophisticated level than that in Vila Brasil. The real battle was not so much for votes but for the hearts and minds of the leadership of the neighborhood association itself. No doubt mindful of the degree of penetration enjoyed by the PDT in the favelas of Rio, Brazil's president José Sarney created the Secretaria Especial de Ação Comunitária (SEAC) in 1986. Ostensibly, SEAC was established to provide favela communities with legal and organizational support and to administer federal assistance programs such as the distribution of free milk tokens. In reality, it was little more than a thinly disguised vehicle for generating votes for President Sarney and his political allies in Rio.

One of the first things SEAC did was to persuade two former presidents of the neighborhood association and longtime PMDB militants to quit their jobs as bus drivers for the private school at the bottom of the hill and instead run the agency in downtown Rio. It then turned its attention to the then president of the neighborhood association. SEAC attempted to recruit the president by paying for a succession of outings by the soccer club to play teams in the interior of the state. These excursions were designed to give the directors of the neighborhood association who had already been recruited an opportunity to "work on" the president, tempting him with offers of relatively secure and lucrative employment. Success would not have guaranteed that the president of the neighborhood association would have changed his political convictions. It would have made it more difficult, however, for him to be openly critical of government policy. Ultimately, the president turned the offer down.[21]

The attempt to seduce the president was just one manifestation of a general tendency for political and ideological differences to divide the directors of the neighborhood association as the election drew nearer. It must be said, however, that despite their many differences of opinion, the individual directors of the neighborhood association remained fairly true to their word in that they kept politics out of neighborhood association business.

Conclusion

The elections in 1986 were eagerly anticipated in the favelas of Vila Brasil and Vidigal, but for very different reasons. In Vila Brasil, the elections meant yet another opportunity to make improvements to the favela through the neighborhood association's participation in time-honored political rituals, rituals that the president of the neighborhood association had learned to manipulate to his and his community's advantage. This was a form of political participation that had brought substantial rewards in the past. There was no logical reason, therefore, to doubt that it would continue to bear fruit in the future.

In Vidigal, the elections meant nothing but trouble, in that the leaders of the neighborhood association were subjected to pressure to use their authority to influence the vote. Because the neighborhood association had long since ceased relying on political contacts to articulate its demands, it was in a fairly good position to resist. In fact, in contrast to the president of Vila Brasil, the leaders of the neighborhood association in Vidigal did all they could to keep favela politics and campaign politics separate.

5

TURNING OUT THE VOTE

At the beginning of this book, I argued that the urban poor have been active, organized, and aggressive participants in the political process. Thus far, however, I have talked almost exclusively about the relationship between the leadership of two neighborhood associations and political elites. What follows, therefore, is an examination of the relationship between the strategies adopted by the two neighborhood associations and the political preferences, attitudes, and beliefs of the population of the two favelas. Before I do this, however, I need to say something about the context and significance of the elections in 1986.

The 1986 Elections

On November 15, 1986, 6,857,163 voters went to the polls in Rio de Janeiro to elect a new governor, two senators, forty-six representatives to the Federal House of Representatives, and seventy representatives to the State Assembly. The elections were by far the most competitive and democratic in the history of Brazilian politics.[1] The elections were also of considerable regional and national significance. The victory of the

Partido Democrático Trabalhista (PDT) in Rio in 1982 served as a spring-board for Leonel Brizola's presidential ambitions. The elections in 1986 represented one more step in this direction. Rio was by far the PDT's most prized possession. Success, therefore, was essential if the party was to maintain its bid to become a national political force.[2]

The elections were also, however, a referendum on the PDT's first four years of public office. The PDT claimed that it had invested more than any other government in the social and educational infrastructure of the state. The opposition, on the other hand, claimed that Brizola's criti-cism of President José Sarney had cost the state in terms of its relation-ship with the federal government and that the PDT had abandoned the middle class in Rio in favor of the perpetrators of urban crime.[3] The opposition in this case took the form of the Aliança Popular Democrá-tica (APD). The APD was a loose and somewhat heterogeneous coalition of twelve different political parties including, among others, the Partido Comunista Brasileira (PCB), the Partido Comunista do Brasil (PCdoB), the Partido da Frente Liberal (PFL), the Partido Trabalhista Brasileiro (PTB), and the Partido do Movimento Democrático Brasileiro (PMDB).[4]

The only other party of note was the Partido dos Trabalhadores (PT). The PT in Rio was not a major political force, however. In fact, in 1985 the party had come in a very poor eighth in the elections for a new mayor. The PT's failure in Rio reflected its elitism and its difficulty in at-tracting the more popular elements of the electorate away from Brizola and the PDT. Unlike the PT in São Paulo, the PT in Rio was dominated by elements of the middle class and by intellectuals, professionals, and radical student groups. As a consequence, the PT often did better in the wealthy residential districts of Zona Sul than in areas of working-class concentration.[5]

The Elections in Vila Brasil and Vidigal

In the ten days prior to the elections on November 15, a stratified, sys-tematic questionnaire survey was conducted of approximately 10 percent of the voting population of the favelas of Vila Brasil and Vidigal.[6] Re-spondents to the survey were asked to identify their candidate of choice for governor, the party to which their candidate belonged, and the reason for their vote. These questions were then repeated for each level of the election, for senator, federal deputy, and state deputy. The results of the survey revealed that the outcome of the elections in the two favelas was in all likelihood very different and that the difference between the voting intentions of the population of Vila Brasil and Vidigal was very much a product of the different strategies adopted by their respective neighborhood associations.

WINNERS AND LOSERS

The distribution of voter preferences in Vila Brasil and Vidigal prior to the elections in November 1986 is detailed in Table 11. This table reveals that there is a significant difference in the voting intentions of the population of the two favelas. In Vidigal, the PDT is clearly the party of preference. Nowhere is this more evident than in the election for governor, where the PDT enjoyed the support of fully 63 percent of all respondents to the survey. While there is a noticeable decline in the level of support for the party at other levels of the election, the PDT still enjoys far greater penetration in the favela than the APD, the second most popular choice.

Table 11 shows that the PDT is also the party of choice in Vila Brasil, but only in the case of the elections for governor, and by a much smaller margin than in Vidigal. In the elections for senator, for federal deputy, and for state deputy, it is the APD that emerges as the party/coalition of choice. In fact, we see from Table 11 that the penetration of the APD in Vila Brasil increases measurably at successively lower levels of the dispute, such that the APD enjoys its highest level of support in the favela in the context of the elections for representatives to the State Assembly.

The results of the survey in Vila Brasil reflect the fact that, in this particular favela, different elections mean very different things. A number of the voting population of Vila Brasil appear to have been impressed by the PDT administration's first four years of office, perhaps by its opposition to federal government policy, but in all likelihood by its efforts to improve the provision of services to the favelas of Zona Oeste. In Vila Brasil, however, support for the PDT's candidate for governor does not carry over to other levels of the dispute. In fact, the more localized

TABLE 11

Political Preferences in Vidigal and Vila Brasil, November 1986

Election	PDT (%)	APD (%)	Other (%)	Undecided (%)
Vidigal				
Governor	63.1	18.0	4.6	14.3
Senator	37.9	18.1	4.4	39.6
Federal deputy	39.0	14.0	6.1	40.9
State deputy	33.2	18.3	5.2	43.3
Vila Brasil				
Governor	40.2	24.4	15.7	19.7
Senator	18.1	25.6	8.7	47.6
Federal deputy	19.7	30.7	8.7	40.9
State deputy	12.6	38.6	7.9	40.9

NOTE: There were 127 respondents to the survey in Vila Brasil and 328 respondents in Vidigal.

the dispute, the greater the influence of those candidates, both past and present, who reached "agreements" with the president of the neighborhood association. It so happens that the most important transactions made by the president of the neighborhood association during his three terms of office were with candidates affiliated with the PMDB, the major partner within the APD.

It should come as no surprise, therefore, that the most popular candidate for a seat in the Federal House of Representatives in Vila Brasil was the old friend of the president of the neighborhood association, Jorge Leite. Almost 13 percent of all respondents to the survey in Vila Brasil and 41 percent of those who chose candidates from the APD for federal deputy said that they were intending to vote for the ex-Chaguista.[7] It is clear, therefore, that the popularity of the APD, relative to its showing in the elections for governor and senator, was in no small part due to the agreement that was reached between Leite and the president of the neighborhood association in 1982.

The importance of this agreement is all the more obvious if one considers that Leite was the candidate of choice of voters with very different political allegiances. In fact, a relatively small number of those who said that they were voting for the ex-Chaguista also said that they were voting for APD candidates at other levels of the election. For example, only 37 percent of those who said that Leite was their candidate for federal deputy said that they were voting for two APD candidates for senator.[8] And, fully 50 percent of those who were intending to vote for Leite said that they were voting for at least one candidate for senator from a party other than the APD.

Thus, although the president of the neighborhood association severed his ties with Leite in 1985 and refused to work for him during the current campaign, a considerable element of the population of Vila Brasil remained faithful to the ex-Chaguista on the strength of what he had done for the favela in the past. This tells us that the loyalties generated by clientelism, such as it is practiced in Vila Brasil, can be extremely resilient. It was, of course, to Leite's advantage that the president of the neighborhood association failed to reach an agreement with a candidate for federal deputy in 1986. Otherwise Leite's showing in the favela might have been less than it was. In the absence of any prompting from the neighborhood association, however, it is more than likely that the population of Vila Brasil voted much as it had done in previous elections.

The fact that Leite had been responsible for paving every road and alleyway in Vila Brasil in 1982 and at one time enjoyed a close working relationship with the president of the neighborhood association meant that he was without doubt the most visible candidate in the favela population's collective memory. In fact, it is likely that the preelectoral survey underestimated the strength of Leite's support in Vila Brasil. There will undoubtedly have been those who could not recall the candidate's name at the time of the survey but who will have voted for Leite on recognizing his name at the ballot box.

If it is no surprise that Leite was the most popular candidate for federal deputy in Vila Brasil it should come as even less of a surprise that Henrique Oswaldo was the most popular candidate for a seat in the State Assembly. Slightly more than 21 percent of all respondents to the survey in Vila Brasil and an impressive 45 percent of all those who identified a candidate for state deputy by name indicated that they were voting for the engineer.[9] This represented 55 percent of all preferences for the APD. Once again, therefore, we see that the popularity of the APD in Vila Brasil was in no small part due to the wheeling and dealing of the president of the neighborhood association.

If we take a look at the demographic characteristics of those who were intending to vote for Oswaldo, we find that there is nothing particularly unusual about this group of voters in relation to the general population of Vila Brasil. Voters for Oswaldo included the young and the old, the educated and the illiterate, and the well-established and more recent arrivals to the favela. In fact, the only feature that distinguishes this group of voters is the fact that they are predominantly female. Only 37 percent of those respondents who said they were planning to vote for Oswaldo were men.[10]

As was the case with Leite, the candidate of the president of the neighborhood association in 1986 also drew his support from a variety of different voter groups in Vila Brasil. Only 41 percent of those who chose Oswaldo as their candidate for state deputy said they were also voting for an APD candidate for federal deputy. Slightly more than 16 percent said they were voting for a candidate for federal deputy from the PDT and 11 percent for a candidate from neither the APD nor the PDT. A further 22 percent of those who had already chosen Oswaldo as their candidate for state deputy said that they were as yet undecided regarding their candidate for federal deputy.[11]

Impressive though these results are, it is important to remember that at the time of the survey, Oswaldo had been taken around the favela but once. In fact, much of the campaigning on the candidate's behalf was yet to be done. It is likely, therefore, that Oswaldo's showing at the ballot box was significantly higher than could be detected in a preelectoral survey. Nevertheless, the fact that Oswaldo had already secured 22 percent of the population of Vila Brasil's votes after having barely been introduced makes the initial assimilation of his name all the more striking. It is also testimony to the power and influence of the president of the neighborhood association in Vila Brasil.

As I have already mentioned, no such inversion was to be found among the voting preferences of the population of Vidigal. In Vidigal, voters opted overwhelmingly and consistently for the PDT, the only variation being in the strength of that support at different levels of the dispute. This suggests that the elections, whether for governor, senator, federal deputy, or state deputy, meant much the same thing to the population of Vidigal and that the neighborhood association had been largely successful in its efforts to protect voters in Vidigal from the type of candidate that is regularly entertained by the president of the neighborhood association in Vila Brasil.

This does not mean that individual candidates achieved no penetration in Vidigal but rather that they were less important and of a different type than those who were successful in Vila Brasil. Indeed, voters in Vidigal clearly had their personal favorites, and in fact, the majority of these were individuals who had been personally involved with the favela in the past. So, for example, slightly more than 11 percent of all respondents to the survey in Vidigal reported that Caó was their candidate for federal deputy, and a further 5 percent said that Renato Vasconcellos was their candidate for state deputy.

In his capacity as state secretary of housing and labor, Caó, of course, had been responsible for the, albeit stalled, appropriation of Vidigal's land. Vasconcellos, on the other hand, had been a longtime friend of the neighborhood association and had overseen the installation of public lighting by LIGHT in the favela in 1981. Both Caó and Vasconcellos were clearly being rewarded for their efforts to improve the provision of urban services to the favela. Theirs was a very different relationship than that which existed between the president of the neighborhood association in Vila Brasil and Leite and Oswaldo, however. Vasconcellos and Caó were popular in Vidigal because they enjoyed the tacit support of the neighborhood association. They enjoyed this support, however, *because* they had not, as yet, abused their positions to further their own political ambitions. In essence, therefore, they were being rewarded for keeping party politics out of the neighborhood association's affairs.[12]

More instructive, perhaps, is the fact that certain candidates fared extremely badly in Vidigal. Alfredo Salamão was state secretary of public works in the Brizola administration and had overseen the program to install sewage systems in a number of favelas in Rio, including Vidigal. Salamão tried campaigning in Vidigal on the basis of what he and the administration had done in the favela, only to be warned off by the president of the neighborhood association. It is interesting to note that Salamão's name was not mentioned by a single respondent to the survey. The other name that was noticeable by its absence was that of Paulo Duque. The ex-Chaguista who once commanded considerable respect in the favela was cited by only 3 percent of all respondents in Vidigal. Thus, if Duque maintained a clientele in the favela it was now a small one. The neighborhood association had effectively guaranteed that his particular brand of politics would never again pay dividends in the area.

The one similarity between voting patterns and individual candidacies in the two favelas is the way that the more popular candidates in Vila Brasil and Vidigal attracted support from voters who would otherwise have opted for a different party. Almost 42 percent of those in Vidigal who chose Caó as their candidate for federal deputy said they had no intention of voting for two PDT candidates for senator. Likewise, only 18 percent of those who were voting for Vasconcellos for state deputy were strictly APD supporters. In fact, 47 percent of Vasconcellos's supporters in the favela were intending to vote for a PDT candidate for federal deputy. Once again, however, the option for either of these two candidates in Vidigal was the fruit of a very different relationship from that which attracted voters to the candidates of the president of the neighborhood association in Vila Brasil.

One final point with regard to the distribution of voting intentions in the two favelas refers to the extreme polarization of the election between the APD and the PDT. Table 11 reveals that relatively few respondents said they were going to vote for parties other than these two, although less so in Vidigal than in Vila Brasil. The PT, in particular, appears to have fared extremely badly in the two favelas. Only 8 percent of all respondents in Vila Brasil and 2 percent of all respondents in Vidigal said that they planned to vote for the PT's candidate for governor in 1986. And, the PT's popularity declined still further at the other levels of the dispute.

POLITICAL PARTY ALLEGIANCE

The fact that individual candidates with the "right" credentials were capable of soliciting support from a variety of different voter groups in Vila Brasil and Vidigal suggests a certain lack of discipline among voters

TABLE 12

Respondents Intending to Vote for Only One Party at Each Level of Elections, November 1986

Political Preference	Vila Brasil (%)	Vidigal (%)
PDT	7.1	26.2
APD	6.3	7.0
Other	1.6	0.3
Split or undecided	85.0	66.5
Total	100.0	100.0

in the two favelas. The tendency for voters to pick and choose between candidates from different parties is not something specific to the favelas, however. The electorate in Brazil is notoriously fickle, largely as a result of the weakness and chronic instability of the political-party system itself. Evidence from the survey suggests, nonetheless, that the extent to which voters indulge themselves in this way is influenced by the social and political context within which such decisions are made.

In particular, the rejection by the leadership of Vidigal of all forms of patronage politics and its efforts to focus the favela population's attention on issues of broader import appear to have produced an electorate that is far more loyal and disciplined than its counterpart in the favela of Vila Brasil. In Vila Brasil, decisions whether to vote for one party's candidate over another are made solely on the basis of a particular individual's ability to deliver before the election. Ideological or party political considerations that might persuade a voter to opt for candidates from a single party play no part in this decision-making process.

Table 12 details the percentage of all respondents to the survey in Vila Brasil and Vidigal who said that they intended to vote for candidates from the same political party at each level of the election. The first thing we notice is that by far the majority of voters in both favelas planned to distribute their votes among candidates from different parties or had not yet decided who they were going to vote for at all levels of the election. There is, however, a significant difference in the pattern of voting behavior in the two favelas. Only 15 percent of respondents in Vila Brasil, as opposed to 33 percent in Vidigal, selected all five candidates (including two candidates for senator) from the same political party.

The difference in the voting behavior of the population of the two favelas can be explained by the presence in Vidigal of a substantial block of voters who are loyal to the PDT. More than 26 percent of all respondents to the survey in Vidigal stated that they were planning to vote for PDT candidates for governor, senator (twice), federal deputy, and state deputy. Therefore, not only is there evidence that the neighborhood association has been successful in its attempts to undermine the basis of patronage politics in Vidigal but that in doing so it has had a hand in the development of political-party loyalties.

There was, of course, substantial support for the PDT's candidate for governor in Vila Brasil. It appears, however, that very few of those who planned to vote for the PDT's Darcy Ribeiro for governor had any intention of voting for PDT candidates at other levels of the dispute. This suggests that the achievements of the Brizola administration's first term of office were associated almost exclusively with the post of state governor. The notion that the future governor's task might be facilitated by a strong party presence in the State Assembly and Federal House of Representatives appears to be a foreign one. After all, elections for senators, federal deputies, and state deputies mean very different things and candidates from other parties that are equally worthy of reward.

Since all respondents to the survey were asked to name both the candidate and the party of their choice for each level of the election, we are in a position to assess the relative weight of political parties versus individual candidacies as a motivation for the vote in the two favelas. Given what we know of the political philosophies of the two favelas and the pattern of voting in the two areas, we might expect that respondents to the survey in Vidigal would be more inclined to identify with a political party than with individual candidates. The opposite should be true of respondents in Vila Brasil, since the political process in that favela revolves almost exclusively around individual candidates. Party politics has little or no place.

Table 13 details the proportion of respondents in each favela who named the party but not the candidate they were going to vote for at

TABLE 13

Percentage of All Preferences Motivated by Party at Each Level, November 1986

Election	Vila Brasil (%)	Vidigal (%)
Governor	0.8	2.4
Senator	10.6	29.1
Federal deputy	10.2	30.8
State deputy	11.8	32.6

each level of the election. With the exception of the election for governor, where all candidates enjoyed a high level of visibility in the media, a far greater proportion of respondents in Vidigal than in Vila Brasil said they were going to vote for a specific party without identifying a candidate by name. We see that slightly more than 32 percent of all respondents in Vidigal, as opposed to only about 12 percent of all respondents in Vila Brasil, said they were going to vote for a candidate from a particular party in the election for state deputy without being able to say who that candidate was. This finding is consistent with the other findings, further suggesting that the neighborhood association in Vidigal had been successful in changing people's understanding of the political process.

If we turn to Table 14, however, we notice that part of the reason for the difference in the relative importance of political parties as motivation for the vote in the two favelas can be explained in terms of differences between the two main parties themselves. We see from Table 14 that, except for the election for governor, a much higher proportion of all PDT voters than APD voters in the two favelas identified with the party and not its candidates. Approximately 70 percent of those who were intending to vote for PDT candidates for state deputy in the two favelas versus 26 percent of those who were going to vote for an APD candidate identified only the party by name.

The differences in the ability of voters for different parties to identify individual candidates by name reflects, in part, an important distinction

TABLE 14
Voter Preferences for the PDT and APD Motivated
by Party at Each Level, November 1986

Election	PDT (%)	APD (%)
Governor	1.9	4.4
Senator	54.1	27.2
Federal deputy	54.2	30.6
State deputy	69.6	26.6

TABLE 15
Percentage of Preferences for the PDT and APD
Motivated by Party Preference at Each Level,
November 1986

	Vila Brasil		Vidigal	
Election	PDT (%)	APD (%)	PDT (%)	APD (%)
Governor	0.0	3.2	2.4	5.1
Senator	15.2	24.6	61.3	28.6
Federal deputy	24.0	10.3	60.2	47.8
State deputy	43.7	10.2	73.4	40.0

between the two major political forces in the election. The PDT was, and still is, a highly centralized party dominated by the considerable presence of Brizola but with few experienced or well-established politicians. The APD, on the other hand, was a rather diffuse and multifarious alliance lacking the single-minded purpose and discipline of the PDT. The APD also included in its ranks a number of ex-Chaguistas whose electoral clout depended on the face-to-face cultivation of political clienteles.

It could be argued, therefore, that the tendency of the PDT voter—and, by implication, the majority of voters in Vidigal—to vote according to party is a function of the paucity of well-known politicians within the PDT and of the formidable and domineering presence of the party's chief rather than anything that is intrinsic to the individual voter.[13] This is at best a partial explanation, however. Table 15 reveals that while the distinction between PDT and APD voters is much the same in the two favelas, it is of a very different magnitude. Thus, we notice from Table 15 that both prospective PDT voters and APD voters in Vidigal are far more likely to name the party but not the candidate of their choice than are their counterparts in Vila Brasil. In other words, if there is a relationship between the organizational structure of the party and a voter's tendency to emphasize the party over the candidate, this relationship is mediated by the social context within which such choices are made.

REASONS FOR THE VOTE

Further evidence of a difference in the meaning and significance of the elections in the two favelas is provided by the justifications that respondents gave for making their choices of candidates. The question itself was open-ended. As a result, there was a wide variety of responses and a number of respondents who failed to come up with any answer at all.[14] There are, nonetheless, some important and telling distinctions to be made between the justifications volunteered by respondents in the two favelas.

It is clear from the nature of the responses to the survey that voters in Vila Brasil and Vidigal were well aware of the national significance of the election for a new governor in that approximately 30 percent of both PDT and APD voters in the two favelas said that they were voting for their respective parties' candidates in support of Brizola or Sarney. As we already know, the proportion of PDT supporters in both favelas greatly outnumbered the proportion of APD supporters for this particular election. The important point, however, is that a significant number of supporters of both parties in the two favelas were voting for the same reason.

Responses to the same question in the context of the elections for senator paint a very different picture. Support for Brizola among PDT voters in both favelas remained very high. Approximately 30 percent of prospective PDT supporters in Vila Brasil and 26 percent in Vidigal cited Brizola by name. Sarney, in the meantime, had already ceased to be an important motivation for APD voters in the two favelas. In fact, only 12 percent of respondents in Vila Brasil and slightly less than 8 percent of respondents in Vidigal said that they were voting for an APD candidate for senator in support of the country's then president. Thus, while a significant proportion of PDT voters chose to support the party's candidates at other levels of the election in light of the national political context, this aspect of the election was already less of an incentive for those who voted for other parties. This change in the meaning of the election was all the more marked in the favela of Vila Brasil, where the APD was now the more popular choice of the two parties. In other words, in Vila Brasil the level of popular support for the APD increased slightly in spite of a decline in the significance of Sarney as a cabo eleitoral.

The elections for representatives to the Federal House of Representatives witnessed the further differentiation between APD and PDT voters in the two favelas. Approximately 24 percent of PDT voters in both Vila Brasil and Vidigal said they were voting for the PDT in support of Brizola, whereas between 7 and 10 percent of those who were intending to vote for the APD in the two favelas justified their choice in terms of their support for Sarney. The elections for representatives to the Federal House of Representatives also witnessed the emergence of a distinction between APD voters in the two favelas. In Vila Brasil, slightly more than 25 percent of those intending to vote for the APD said they were opting for the party at this level because of personal contact with a politician or with someone responsible for promoting a candidate's campaign. Many respondents said they were voting because they had been given work by a candidate, because they had been blessed by a visit from a candidate, or because a candidate had made them certain promises. Others said they were voting because their church, the local samba block, or the president of the neighborhood association had told them to.

Voters intending to choose Leite as their candidate for federal deputy volunteered similar information. One respondent said she was going to vote for Leite because she supported Sarney; another because the ex-Chaguista had always "sided with the poor." The vast majority, however, cited more personal and concrete reasons. One person said she was voting for him because Leite had gotten her a job; two others because his candidacy was being backed by the local samba block. Almost 40 percent said they were voting for him explicitly because of what he had done for the favela back in 1982.

The reasons respondents in Vila Brasil gave for their choices in the election for federal deputy were, therefore, very much the product of the political organization of that favela. They reflect a popular vision of the political process whereby votes are commodities to be sold to the highest bidder and whereby candidates who make good on their promises are promptly rewarded. This does not mean, however, that voters in Vidigal were unwilling to reward candidates for what they had done for the favela. For example, fully 53 percent of those who said they were intending to vote for Caó alluded to the work he had overseen in his capacity as state secretary of housing and labor. The relationship between Caó and his constituents in Vidigal was very different from the relationship between Leite and his constituents in Vila Brasil, however.

First, Leite had arranged for the paving of Vila Brasil *on condition* that the favela would then vote for him. Caó, on the other hand, had overseen the appropriation process in the understanding that no one would be obliged to support his candidacy. Try as they may, of course, the leaders of the neighborhood association could not prevent people from voting on the basis of what Caó was doing in the favela. They could, however, make sure that the provision of public works projects was not *dependent* on delivering the vote in Vidigal. Second, Caó's popularity in Vidigal was also clearly a function of his association with the PDT and an administration that had done something, albeit not much, about the paucity of urban services in the favelas. Because of this, 30 percent of those who said that Caó was their candidate for federal deputy also said that they were voting for him specifically in support of Brizola.

As one might expect, the differences between PDT and APD voters and between voters in Vila Brasil and Vidigal were even more marked for the election for representatives to the State Assembly. Brizola continued to be an important motivation for supporting the PDT at this level of the election in that slightly more than 31 percent of prospective PDT voters in Vila Brasil and almost 28 percent of prospective PDT voters in Vidigal said they were choosing the party on the basis of their support for its leader. Meanwhile, support for Sarney among those intending to vote for the APD stabilized in both favelas at around 6 percent. Once again, however, the most significant difference in the voting behavior of the two favelas can be traced to the policies of the president of the neighborhood association in Vila Brasil. Almost 43 percent of those who were planning to vote for the APD in Vila Brasil cited reasons associated with clientelist politics, and by far the majority of these responses (90 percent) were associated with the candidacy of Oswaldo.

Seven different reasons were given for voting for the candidate of the president of the neighborhood association that year: support for Sarney, support for the PMDB, the candidate's concern for the contents of the new constitution, the candidate's recent visit to the community, the candidate's good looks and cheery disposition, the candidate's gift to the favela, and support for Oswaldo's candidacy by the president of the neighborhood association. The final reason was by far the most widely cited. In fact, fully 52 percent of those who said they were going to vote for Oswaldo said they were simply following the president's advice.[15]

The disposition of the residents of Vila Brasil to support candidates who were willing to pay for votes reveals the internal dynamic of clientelism in Vila Brasil. It illustrates how popular experience has fostered an approach to politics that looks to take advantage of the immediate opportunities that the process provides. In Vila Brasil, this disposition was responsible for the popularity of the APD, which enjoyed its highest level of support in the elections for state deputy.

Conclusion

The results of the preelectoral survey of voting intentions in the favelas of Vila Brasil and Vidigal show that there is a strong relationship between the way a favela is organized and the way that people think about the political process. This relationship manifests itself in a number of different ways. One way is in terms of whom people support at the ballot box. The neighborhood association in Vila Brasil pursues its interests by making the best of what limited opportunities clientelist politics provides by exchanging votes for favors. This strategy has been responsible for some major improvements to the physical infrastructure of the favela over the past ten years, and as a consequence, there is no shortage of individuals who are more than willing to follow the president's advice. Thus, for certain types of elections, the most successful candidates in Vila Brasil are those who are willing to buy their way into public office.

The influence of the neighborhood association in Vila Brasil goes beyond telling people who they should vote for, however. The neighborhood association also tells people *how* they should vote in terms of what they should look for in a candidate. Therefore, while in any given election it is rare for the president of the neighborhood association to promote more than one candidate, his vision of the political process colors every choice that is made by those who follow his leadership. Voters in Vila Brasil have a tendency, therefore, to choose candidates who have touched their personal lives in some material way. It also means that voters in Vila Brasil have a tendency to pick and choose among any number of different candidates from any number of different parties. It just so happens that in recent years the president of the neighborhood association has reached agreements with politicians from the PMDB. This has nothing to do with party loyalty, however.

The leaders of the neighborhood association in Vidigal, on the other hand, no longer depend on the politics of favors since they have devised alternative and equally effective means of persuading the various arms of the state to invest in the favela. The leaders of the neighborhood association have also, therefore, eliminated the need to solicit the help of candidates of the kind that are regularly entertained by the president of Vila Brasil.

On one level, this has brought an end to the reign of the likes of Duque, who once held sway in the favela. On another, it has blunted successive attempts by the PDT to use universal entitlement programs as a form of political blackmail. Finally, the transformation of the neighborhood association in Vidigal has divorced the issue of who to vote for from the day-to-day concerns of the favela. Instead, the leaders of the neighborhood association are able to promote the idea that political parties are institutions that are essential to the process of social and political change. And while voters in Vidigal are more likely than not to choose between candidates from different parties, they are far more likely than their counterparts in the favela of Vila Brasil to entertain the idea of voting for candidates from a single slate.

CONCLUSION

In January 1978 state government officials failed in an attempt to force three hundred or so families to abandon their homes in Vidigal. In November 1982, state government trucks paved every road and alleyway in Vila Brasil. Two seemingly unrelated and insignificant events in two of Rio's five hundred or so favelas. The evidence presented in this book suggests otherwise, however. Indeed, it suggests that not only are these two events intimately related but that they in fact tell us a great deal about the different strategies and demands of the urban poor. Most important of all, however, they tell us that the population of Rio's favelas has exercised a considerable degree of control over both its participation in the political process and its relationship with political elites.

The Manipulation of Consent

Since the beginning of this century, where the urban poor could and could not live in Rio has been a decision for the most part beyond their control. Driven from low-cost housing in the center of the city in the early 1900s, Rio's rapidly expanding urban proletariat had little choice but to provide for its own accommodation in what subsequently became the favelas. Since that time, the favelas have sometimes been tolerated but more often than not brutally repressed, depending on wider political circumstances.

Wider political circumstances have corresponded fairly closely to cycles of democratic and authoritarian rule. Thus, we find that the first attempts to consolidate the favelas in Rio began in the late 1940s with the end of the Estado Novo and ended some twenty years later with the return to military rule. The correspondence between periods of state tolerance toward the favelas and periods of democratic rule is, of course, no accident. It is precisely during such times that members of the local political elite are most likely to turn to the favelas as a source of political support. Unfortunately, when the urban poor could and could not vote has also been a decision largely beyond their control such that in times of wholesale favela removal the population of Rio's favelas has been denied the use of what is, without doubt, its most powerful political weapon.

Even during periods of democratic rule, however, we find that the population of Rio's favelas has been persuaded to engage in what have been considered "appropriate" forms of political behavior. In other words, by restricting political-party competition and by undermining independent bases of popular organization in the favelas, the state has sought to guarantee that the urban poor participate in the political process in ways that serve the interests of political elites.

Appropriate forms of political behavior have for the most part meant voting for elitist candidates for public office in return for some form of public good whether it be a job, a set of shirts for the local soccer club, or the promise of a politician's ear. The effect of this relationship has been twofold. First, it has led to the fairly widespread emergence of political institutions in the favelas, of which neighborhood associations are but one example, that are geared toward facilitating precisely this type of transaction. Second, it has generated an understanding among the urban poor that politics is primarily, if not exclusively, about the granting and denial of personal political favors.

Weapons of the Weak

It would be wrong, however, to suggest that popular political participation and organization in Rio have been determined solely by the actions and decisions of politicians and administrators, just as it would be a mistake to suggest that the population of Rio's favelas has stood idly by and accepted its fate. At each juncture, the urban poor in Rio have stubbornly resisted attempts both to do away with the favelas and to interfere with favela politics, to the extent that the actions and decisions of political elites themselves bear the unmistakable imprint of the favela population's own strategies and demands.

In this book we have examined the nature and implications of two such strategies. In the case of Vila Brasil we saw that the president of the neighborhood association, while accepting the premise of clientelist politics, has learned to manipulate his relationship with politicians and administrators to the favela's maximum advantage. He has done this in four ways: by cultivating his own network of friends and contacts in local government and political-party offices in downtown Rio, by convincing candidates for public office that he commands a large number of votes, by inviting candidates to submit competitive bids for the favela's exclusive support, and, finally, by demanding that payment be made in full before the election.

The outcome of this strategy has been twofold: an immediate and dramatic improvement in the quality of life of the population of Vila Brasil and the emergence of a powerful, well-organized, and extremely efficient neighborhood association that is tailored to exigencies of clientelist politics.

This strategy has also, however, meant that the population of Vila Brasil has, over the past ten years or so, voted on a regular basis for candidates for public office who in one way or another are willing to buy their way into public office. In essence, this has meant voting for candidates who feel comfortable exploiting the misery and uncertainty of favela life and who, therefore, have little or no interest in the elimination of current levels of socioeconomic and political inequality.

The president of the neighborhood association is well aware of the consequences of his particular political strategy because of the class of politicians that descends on Vila Brasil around election time and because his strategy is the basis of considerable acrimony and conflict between himself and the local leadership of Federação de Associações de Favelas do Estado do Rio de Janeiro (FAFERJ) and the Pastoral de Favelas. The president is equally aware, however, that Vila Brasil is one of the best-served favelas in the region and that his advice is much sought after by other favela leaders in Zona Oeste.

Finally, the president is also well aware that his success over the past ten years or so has been achieved with the minimum of effort and involvement on behalf of the population of Vila Brasil and without once compromising the autonomy of the neighborhood association. And it is the apolitical, or, rather, antipolitical, nature of his presidency that perhaps more than anything has won him the unswerving and unconditional support of a large proportion of the population of Vila Brasil.

In the case of Vidigal, on the other hand, we saw how a favela that had once depended on clientelism to articulate its political interests turned its back on this system. It did so because the attempt to remove the favela from its present site in Zona Sul in 1977 exposed it to the limitations of clientelist politics and brought it into contact with other favela communities and nongovernment organizations that were mounting a challenge to authoritarian rule.

Subsequently, what emerged as the leadership of the favela took it upon itself to rethink the way the neighborhood association went about its business. This meant that instead of going cap in hand to politicians and begging for favors, the leadership of Vidigal now made it difficult for the various municipal, state, and federal government agencies not to improve the provision of basic urban services in the favela.

The outcome, much as in Vila Brasil, has been an immediate and dramatic improvement in the quality of life of the population of the favela and the emergence of a powerful, well-organized, and efficient neighborhood association. Unlike Vila Brasil, however, the neighborhood association in Vidigal is tailored not to the exigencies of clientelism but to the exigencies of combating and blunting the effect of all forms of patronage politics. This means that the leadership of the neighborhood association in Vidigal spends a great deal of its time soliciting the financial backing of various government agencies while at the same time making sure that such offers of assistance are made in the understanding that they will not necessarily translate into votes.

The efforts of the leadership of the neighborhood association have thus far cost the favela little in terms of its ability, relative to other favelas, to improve the provision of basic services in Vidigal. Rather, these efforts have brought an end to the more traditional forms of electioneering in the favela and have done much to sever the popular association between public works and the vote.

Finally, these efforts have also enabled the population of the favela to consider a set of very different political issues. Instead of voting for candidates solely on the basis of what they have done in the favela, residents in Vidigal are now more likely to consider the merits of politicians and political parties that speak to their concern for a set of more general issues.

Good Favela/Bad Favela

The neighborhood associations in Vila Brasil and Vidigal are excellent illustrations of the different strategies that have been adopted by the urban poor in Rio. On the one hand, the neighborhood association in Vila Brasil has pursued its interests by upping the political ante and by taking politicians on at their own game. The neighborhood association in Vidigal, on the other hand, has pursued its interests by attempting to change the rules of the political game itself.

Somewhat ironically, however, both the neighborhood association in Vila Brasil and that in Vidigal owe their current position and, to a large extent, their past success to the mobilization of popular protest against the military in Rio de Janeiro in the late 1970s and early 1980s: Vidigal because nongovernment organizations involved with the popular movement helped the population of the favela defend itself against the threat of removal in 1977; Vila Brasil because the Pastoral de Favelas, itself a product of the events in Vidigal, was instrumental in forcing the former president of the neighborhood association to step down and for new elections to be held.

Therefore, different though their actions and the consequences of their actions may be, the favelas of Vila Brasil and Vidigal are much the products of the same political moment and of the attempt, not just by the population of Rio's favelas, to end what is now almost a century of repression, manipulation, and neglect. Of course, the days of the popular movement and of large-scale popular protest in Brazil are long gone, meaning that the urban poor have, once again, been left to their own devices. One day, however, their toil and suffering will, I hope, prove not to have been in vain.

Appendix: Methodology

Selecting Two Favelas

The selection and study of two favelas representing common yet contrasting strategies of popular organization in Rio presented a set of difficult and unique methodological circumstances. First, apart from a small number of case studies that I did not wish to replicate, very little published information regarding the organizational characteristics of individual favela communities in Rio was available. It was soon obvious, therefore, that I would be in a position to make such a selection only if I was familiar with the physical and political reality of a whole range of favela types.

This presented me with the considerable problem of access. Most people in Rio have never and would never set foot in the favelas. And while there is no doubt that the level of violence in the favelas is sensationalized in the local press, it would be extremely unwise for a stranger to wander into a favela unaccompanied or unannounced. Furthermore, without prior contact or introduction, any form of meaningful research would be well nigh impossible.

Faced with such difficulties, I spent the first six weeks of my stay in Rio examining back copies of the *Jornal do Brasil*. This provided me with invaluable background information on the number, distribution, and general ecological characteristics of Rio's five hundred or so favelas. More important, however, it enabled me to identify and contact organizations that were closely involved with the population of the favelas. The most important of these organizations were the Federação de Associações de Favelas do Estado do Rio de Janeiro (FAFERJ) and the Pastoral de Favelas. Both FAFERJ and the Pastoral de Favelas were to become invaluable sources of information during the course of my stay in Rio. It was the Pastoral de Favelas, however, that granted me access to such areas.

Between mid March and late June of 1986 I was fortunate in that I was invited by agents of the Pastoral de Favelas to be their guest at numerous meetings throughout the region. Some of these were statewide favela neighborhood association federation meetings, some were meetings of favela neighborhood associations of a particular area, and others were simply meetings in individual favelas. My attendance at these meetings provided me with insight into the type of issues that were being discussed, the different ways that the leadership of the favelas went about its business, the role of the church and other outside agencies, and, of course, the physical hardships of favela life. Most important of all, however, my attendance at these meetings brought me into almost daily contact with leaders of a wide variety of favelas in Rio, many of whom became my close friends and confidants.

By the end of May I felt confident that I knew enough about the favelas in general to be able to select two that represented alternative forms of political organization among the urban poor. These favelas were Vila Brasil and Vidigal. Of course, the selection of two favelas that are supposedly representative of a group of more than five hundred is highly problematic. It is so in that the selection process depends on the issue of interest and in that capturing or "modeling" the complex diversity of favela life in Rio is clearly impossible. Therefore, it would be wrong to suggest that Vila Brasil and Vidigal are pure representations of the different types of political organization in the favelas or that there is no overlap between the two. Having said this, however, the favelas are representative of distinctions that are recognized both in the academic literature on popular organizations in Rio and, more important, by the leadership of the favelas itself.

Field Research

Gaining access to the two favelas was relatively easy by means of the contacts I had made at the Pastoral de Favelas. Gaining access to reliable information from the residents of the two favelas was far more difficult, however. In Vidigal, I was fortunate in that I was granted the opportunity to teach English to a group of schoolchildren in the favela. I say fortunate, in that it allowed me to get to know a large number of people in the favela in a relatively short period of time and it earned me the trust of at least a few of the leaders of the neighborhood association. I can say with all honesty, however, that it was my performance on the soccer field more than anything else that guaranteed the success of my research in Vidigal. For it was not until I scored a couple of goals for the favela's soccer team at a local Pastoral de Favelas meeting that a director of the neighborhood association who was to become an invaluable source of information would give me the time of day!

In Vila Brasil, the problem was of a very different nature in that, once I had been introduced, I had absolutely no trouble in persuading the president of the neighborhood association to talk about his exploits. In fact, the president delighted in telling anyone who would listen about the various different ways he had persuaded politicians to part with government money. Realizing that the president might be tempted to exaggerate his role in the political process, I was then forced to verify with others who had been present at the time everything that he told me. Apart from a few minor details and embellishments, however, his accounts turned out to be extremely reliable.[1]

Over time, of course, my almost constant presence in the two favelas became so routine that I was privy to all kinds of meetings, events, and crises. And, in fact, most of what I learned during my six months in Vila Brasil and Vidigal was the fruit not of formal interviews but of casual conversations and day-to-day encounters. Indeed, it was only at the very end of my stay in Rio that I made any attempt to record interviews with the major players in the two favelas, to the extent that these interviews were, in effect, reiterations of discussions that had already taken place.

Administering the Survey

If selecting and gaining access to the two favelas presented their own difficulties, the administration of a preelectoral survey in Vila Brasil and Vidigal was far more problematic. Originally, my intention had been to use official election returns to determine whether there were any differences in the voting habits of the population of the two areas that could be attributed to differences in political organization. In the event, however, this proved impossible in that the smallest electoral districts in Rio were still considerably larger than either Vila Brasil or Vidigal. The results of the election in the two favelas would, therefore, have been mixed in with the results of the election from the surrounding areas. This was especially true in Vidigal, where the favela rubbed shoulders with luxury apartments and houses belonging to occupants of a very different social class. Furthermore, according to new electoral legislation passed that year, voters could choose where in the city they were going to vote. There was no guarantee, therefore, that the residents of the two favelas in fact voted in the electoral districts that corresponded to their particular area.

Faced with these problems, I decided instead to conduct a preelectoral survey in the two favelas. Of course, any number of problems were associated with such a survey, not the least of which was the issue of whether or not respondents would reveal the way they were about to vote. This issue was especially relevant in a country that had just seen the end of twenty years of authoritarian rule, during which time popular political discussion, participation, and organization had been severely curtailed.

There were two reasons to believe that this would not be a significant threat to the validity of the survey, however. First, I had been a frequent visitor to both favelas for nearly six months, such that almost everyone knew of me and of my research project. Second, the neighborhood associations in both favelas granted me permission to conduct the survey on condition that I employed residents of the two favelas as my research assistants.

Employing residents as research assistants had its advantages and disadvantages. It was an advantage in that, for the most part, I could employ individuals I already knew and trusted and in that it minimized the likelihood that respondents in the two favelas would be reluctant to reveal their election preferences.[2] It was a disadvantage, however, in that many of my research assistants had left school long before completing primary school. This meant that, while they were more than capable of following my instructions, the questionnaire itself had to be relatively simple and straightforward. It also meant that I had to accompany each research assistant through the interview process until I was confident that they knew what they were doing, and that I ended up supervising approximately 70 percent of all of the questionnaires that were administered in the two favelas.

The second problem associated with conducting a preelectoral survey in the two favelas was logistical. I had decided that the survey should sample 10 percent of the voting population in both favelas and that it should be conducted as to close to election day as possible. This meant approximately 450 interviews in the space of just one week. The sheer enormity of the task was, therefore, a major consideration in the design of the questionnaire and of the procedure by which it was to be administered.

On the other hand, there were also distinct advantages to the survey. First, it allowed for a far greater degree of control over differences in the demographic characteristics of the two favelas, to the extent that such differences existed. Second, the survey allowed me to examine voting sequences for individual respondents, which would not have been possible if I had relied on official election returns. Third, the survey allowed me to ask voters not only how they were going to vote but also why they were going to vote, an issue of obvious significance for a comparison of the two favelas in this study.

The most time-consuming aspect of the survey involved drawing the sample. To maximize the amount of control I could exercise over the sampling process, to minimize the chance of sampling error, and to make it as simple as possible, the selection of interviewees was split into two separate stages. The first stage involved the division of the two favelas into sections of roughly equal size. Because of its greater size, however, this stage in the sampling process proved far more problematic in Vidigal than in Vila Brasil.

Vidigal was divided into eight sections, each with roughly equal numbers of dwelling units according to what turned out to be somewhat inaccurate maps from the Secretaria Municipal de Planejamento. Each of the eight research assistants in Vidigal was then given an area. Each research assistant systematically chose every fourth house along each road and alleyway in that area. The total number of dwellings that were selected in Vidigal came to 328, giving a total of approximately 1,300 dwellings in the entire favela. Because it worked out that some sections had more houses than others, the eight sections were then redrawn accordingly.

The same method was used in Vila Brasil, where a total of approximately 500 dwellings rendered a sample of 128. The logic behind this sampling method was as follows. According to the 1980 census for Rio de Janeiro, there were on average two adults of voting age per household. This ratio was likely to be higher, however, for households in working-class neighborhoods such as Vila Brasil and Vidigal. Therefore, to obtain a 10 percent sample of the voting population of the two favelas, it was necessary to sample 25 percent of all households, within which only one respondent of voting age would be interviewed.

The second stage of the sampling process involved the selection of the 456 individual respondents in the two favelas. The sample was stratified by age and by sex according to the distribution of these variables among the population of the state of Rio de Janeiro. Thus, each research assistant was instructed to select the same proportion of respondents by age and sex according to a predetermined sequence of categories.[3]

This meant that each research assistant would start by entering the first house on the list of dwellings that had been identified in the first stage of the sampling process and by asking if there was a male in the house who would be over forty years of age on the day of the election. If such an individual existed, he was then informed of the nature of the project and told that the research assistant would return one week before the election to conduct the interview. Finally, he was asked which days of the week and which times of the day he was most likely to be at home such that the research assistants in each area could minimize the amount of time they spent hunting down respondents. On completion of this process, the number of the house, the age and sex of the respondent, and the day and time of day of the interview were recorded on a sheet that was itself ordered by categories of sex and age.

At the next house the research assistant would ask if there was anyone living there that occupied the next age and sex category on the list. If no one of that particular age and sex was there, the research assistant would proceed to the next category until a suitable respondent had been identified. At the next house the research assistant would then return to the top of the list until the sequence of respondents had been restored. This sequence of categories was ordered such that, if followed according to instructions, it would produce the appropriate proportions of men and women of different ages. The three age groups that were used were (1) less than thirty, (2) between thirty and thirty-nine, and (3) forty years of age or older. Age was classified thus to ensure simplicity and to minimize the likelihood that respondents would lie about their age.

As you can well imagine, the selection of respondents in the two favelas took a considerable amount of time, energy, and patience on behalf of myself and my research assistants. In the end, however, it made the task of conducting 456 interviews in the week before the elections of November 15 much easier, such that only a handful of individuals in the two favelas refused to answer the questionnaire.

Notes

NOTES TO THE INTRODUCTION

1. The classic statements in this regard are by David Collier, *Squatters and Oligarchs: Authoritarian Rule and Policy Change in Peru* (Baltimore, Md.: Johns Hopkins University Press, 1976); Wayne Cornelius, *Politics and the Migrant Poor in Mexico City* (Stanford, Calif.: Stanford University Press, 1975); Henry Dietz, *Poverty and Problem-Solving Under Military Rule* (Austin, Tex.: University of Texas Press, 1980); and Susan Eckstein, *The Poverty of Revolution: The State and the Urban Poor in Mexico* (Princeton, N.J.: Princeton University Press, 1977).

2. For research on this issue, see Cathy Schneider, "Mobilization at the Grassroots: Shantytowns and Resistance in Authoritarian Chile," *Latin American Perspectives* 18(68) (1991): 92–112; Juan M. R. Saiz, "Urban Struggles and Their Consequences," in Joe Foweraker and Ann L. Craig, eds., *Popular Movements and Political Change in Mexico* (Boulder, Colo.: Lynne Reinner, 1990), pp. 234–246; Susan Stokes, "Politics and Latin America's Urban Poor: Reflections from a Lima Shantytown," *Latin American Research Review* 26(2) (1991): 75–101; and Carlos Vilas, "El Sujeto Social de la Insurreccíon Popular: La Revolución Sandinista," *Latin American Research Review* 20(1) (1985): 119–147.

3. This book is the fruit of a year's field research in Rio de Janeiro in 1986 and of four subsequent visits between 1987 and 1992. For further details refer to the Appendix.

4. For the different elements of the popular movement, see Sonia E. Alvarez, *Engendering Democracy in Brazil* (Princeton, N.J.: Princeton University Press, 1990); Renato R. Boschi, *A Arte da Associação, Política de Base e Democracia no Brasil* (São Paulo: Edições Vértice, 1987); Ralph Della ʻCava, "A

Igreja e a Abertura, 1974–1985," in Paulo J. Krischke and Scott Mainwaring, eds., *A Igreja nas Bases em Tempo de Transição* (Pôrto Alegre, Brazil: CEDEC, 1986), pp. 13–45; Eli Diniz, "Favela: Associativismo e Participação Social," in Renato R. Boschi, ed., *Movimentos Coletivos no Brasil Urbano* (Rio de Janeiro: Zahar, 1983), pp. 27–74; Margaret Keck, "The New Unionism in the Brazilian Transition," in Alfred Stepan, ed., *Democratizing Brazil* (New York: Oxford University Press, 1989), pp. 252–296; idem, "Democratization and Dissension: The Formation of the Workers' Party," *Politics and Society* 15(1) (1986–87): 67–95; Carmen Cinira Macedo, *Tempo de Genesis: O Povo das Comunidades Eclesiais de Base* (São Paulo: Brasiliense, 1986); Scott Mainwaring, "Grassroots Popular Movements and the Struggle for Democracy: Nova Iguaçu," in Stepan, *Democratizing Brazil*, pp. 168–204; and Maria Hermínia Tavares de Almeida, "Novo Sindicalismo and Politics in Brazil," in John D. Wirth, Edson O. Nunes, and Thomas E. Bogenschild, eds., *State and Society in Brazil: Continuity and Change* (Boulder, Colo.: Westview Press, 1987), pp. 147–177.

5. The theoretical framework for this prediction was borrowed from analyses of the so-called new social movements in Europe. Most influential were the works of Jordi Borja, *Movimentos Sociales Urbanos* (Buenos Aires: Ediçiones SIAP, 1975); Manuel Castells, *City, Class and Power* (London: Macmillan, 1978); idem, *The Urban Question* (London: Edward Arnold, 1977); and Jean Lojkine, *Le Marxisme, l'État et la Question Urbaine* (Paris: PUF, 1977). For a sample of works influenced by neo-Marxist theory, see Maria da Glória Gohn, *Reivindicações Populares Urbanas: Um Estudo Sobre as Sociedades de Amigos de Bairro de São Paulo* (São Paulo: Edições Cortes, 1981); José Álvaro Moisés, ed., *Cidade, Povo e Poder* (Rio de Janeiro: Paz e Terra, 1981); idem, ed., *Contradições Urbanas e Movimentos Sociais* (Rio de Janeiro: Paz e Terra, 1977); and Maria Helena Moreira Alves, "Grassroots Organizations, Trade Unions and the Church: A Challenge to Controlled Abertura in Brazil," *Latin American Perspectives* 2(11) (1984): 73–102.

6. For an analysis of the political sociology of postauthoritarian Brazil, see Aspásia Camargo and Eli Diniz, eds., *Continuidade e Mudança no Brasil da Nova República* (Rio de Janeiro: Edições Vértice and IUPERJ, 1989); Eli Diniz, Renato R. Boschi, and Renato Lessa, eds., *Modernização e Consolidação Democrática no Brasil: Dilemas da Nova República* (Rio de Janeiro: Edições Vértice and IUPERJ, 1989); Frances Hagopian and Scott Mainwaring, "Democracy in Brazil: Problems and Prospects," *World Policy Journal* 4(3) (1987): 485–514; Bolivar Lamounier and Raquel Meneguello, *Partidos Políticos e Consolidação Democrática, o Caso Brasileira* (São Paulo: Brasiliense, 1986); and José Álvaro Moisés and J. A. Guilhon Albuquerque, eds., *Dilemas da Consolidação da Democracia* (São Paulo: Paz e Terra, 1989).

7. For the transition in Brazil, see Eli Diniz, "A Transição Polítíca no Bra-

sil: Uma Avaliação da Dinâmica da Abertura," *Dados* 28(3) (1985): 329–346; Silvio R. Duncan Baretta and John Markoff, "Brazil's *Abertura*: From What to What?" in James M. Malloy and Mitchell A. Seligson, eds., *Authoritarians and Democrats* (Pittsburgh, Pa.: University of Pittsburgh Press, 1987), pp. 43–65; Scott Mainwaring, "The Transition to Democracy in Brazil," *Journal of Interamerican Studies and World Affairs* 28 (1986): 149–179; Luciano Martins, "The 'Liberalization' of Authoritarian Rule in Brazil," in Guillermo O'Donnell, Philippe Schmitter, and Laurence Whitehead, eds., *Transitions from Authoritarian Rule: Latin America* (Baltimore, Md.: Johns Hopkins University Press, 1986), pp. 72–94; Maria Helena Moreira Alves, *State and Opposition in Military Brazil* (Austin: University of Texas Press, 1985); and Margaret J. Sarles, "Maintaining Political Control Through Parties: The Brazilian Strategy," *Comparative Politics* 15 (1982): 41–72.

8. The notion of a weak civil society and a strong state is a common one in Brazilian political sociology. For example, see Maria do Carmo Campello de Souza, *Estado e Partidos Políticos no Brasil (1930 a 1964)* (São Paulo: Alfa-Ômega, 1976); Youseff Cohen, *The Manipulation of Consent* (Pittsburgh, Pa.: University of Pittsburgh Press, 1989); Luciano Martins, *Estado Capitalista e Burocracia no Brasil Pós-64* (Rio de Janeiro: Paz e Terra, 1985); Fernando Rezende, "O Crescimento (Descontrolado) da Intervenção Governamental na Economia Brasileira," in Olavo Brasil de Lima, Jr., and Sérgio H. Abranches, eds., *As Origens da Crise: Estado Autoritário e Planejamento no Brasil* (São Paulo: Edições Vértice, 1987), pp. 214–252; Philippe Schmitter, *Interest Conflict and Political Change in Brazil* (Stanford, Calif.: Stanford University Press, 1971); and Alfred Stepan, "State Power and the Strength of Civil Society in the Southern Cone of Latin America," in Peter Evans, Dietrich Rueschemeyer, and Theda Skocpol, eds., *Bringing the State Back In* (Cambridge: Cambridge University Press, 1985), pp. 317–343.

9. For industrialization and, in particular, the role of the state in Brazil, see Werner Baer, Isaac Kerstenetsky, and Anibal Villela, "The Changing Role of the State in the Brazilian Economy," *World Development* 1 (1973): 23–34; Fernando Henrique Cardoso, *Empresário Industrial e Desenvolvimento Econômico no Brasil* (São Paulo: Difel, 1964); Eli Diniz, *Empresário, Estado e Capitalismo no Brasil: 1930–1945* (Rio de Janeiro: Paz e Terra, 1978); and Peter Evans, *Dependent Development* (Princeton, N.J.: Princeton University Press, 1979).

10. This is not to suggest that the state had no impact on working-class politics in the developed world. For example, see the various essays in Ira Katznelson and Aristide Zolberg, eds., *Working-Class Formation: Nineteenth-Century Patterns in Western Europe and the United States* (Princeton, N.J.: Princeton University Press, 1986).

11. For a discussion of the form and logic of clientelism, see Peter Flynn, "Class, Clientelism and Coercion: Some Mechanisms of Internal Dependency Con-

trol," *Journal of Commonwealth and Comparative Politics* 12(2) (1974): 138–156; Samuel Huntington and Joan Nelson, *No Easy Choice: Political Participation in Developing Countries* (New Haven, Conn.: Yale University Press, 1976); Robert Kaufmann, "The Patron–Client Concept and Macro-Politics: Prospects and Problems," *Comparative Studies in Society and History* 16 (1974): 284–308; René Lemarchand and Keith Legg, "Political Clientelism and Development: A Preliminary Analysis," *Comparative Politics* 4 (1972): 149–178; Joan Nelson, *Access to Power: Politics and the Urban Poor in Developing Nations* (Princeton, N.J.: Princeton University Press, 1979); Luis Roniger, *Hierarchy and Trust in Mexico and Brazil* (New York: Praeger, 1990); Frances Rothstein, "The Class Basis of Patron–Client Relations," *Latin American Perspectives* 6(2) (1979): 25–35; and James C. Scott, "The Erosion of Patron–Client Relations and Social Change in Southeast Asia," *Journal of Asian Studies* 32(1) (1972): 5–37.

12. For a discussion of populism as an analytical concept, see Michael L. Conniff, "Introduction: Towards a Comparative Definition of Populism," in Michael L. Conniff, ed., *Latin American Populism in Comparative Perspective* (Albuquerque: University of New Mexico Press, 1982), pp. 3–30. For a discussion of the differences and similarities between clientelism and populism, see Nicos Mouzelis, "On the Concept of Populism: Populist and Clientelist Modes of Incorporation in Semiperipheral Polities," *Politics and Society* 14(3) (1985): 329–348.

13. See, for example, Geert A. Banck, "Poverty, Politics and the Shaping of Urban Space: A Brazilian Example," *International Journal of Urban and Regional Research* 10(4) (1986): 522–540; Paul Cammack, "Clientelism and Military Government in Brazil," in Christopher Clapham, ed., *Private Patronage and Public Power* (New York: St. Martin's Press, 1982), pp. 53–75; Ruth B. Collier, "Popular Sector Incorporation and Political Supremacy: Regime Evolution in Brazil and Mexico," in Sylvia A. Hewlett and Richard S. Weinert, eds., *Brazil and Mexico: Patterns in Late Development* (Philadelphia, Pa.: Institute for the Study of Human Issues, 1982), pp. 57–109; Michael L. Conniff, *Urban Politics in Brazil: The Rise of Populism, 1925–1945* (Pittsburgh, Pa.: University of Pittsburgh Press, 1981); Eli Diniz, *Voto e Máquina Política: Clientelismo e Patronagem no Rio de Janeiro* (Rio de Janeiro: Paz e Terra, 1982); Kenneth P. Erickson, *The Brazilian Corporative State and Working-Class Politics* (Berkeley, Calif.: University of California Press, 1977); Richard Graham, *Patronage and Politics in Nineteenth-Century Brazil* (Stanford, Calif.: Stanford University Press, 1990); Octávio Ianni, *A Formação do Estado Populista na América Latina* (Rio de Janeiro: Civilização Brasileira, 1975); Victor Nunes Leal, *Coronelismo, Enxada e Voto: O Município e o Regime Representativo no Brasil* (São Paulo: Alfa-Ômega, 1975); Kenneth S. Mericle, "Corporatist Control of the Brazilian Working Class: Authoritarian Brazil Since

1964," in James M. Malloy, ed., *Authoritarianism and Corporatism in Latin America* (Pittsburgh, Pa.: University of Pittsburgh Press, 1977), pp. 303–338; Eul-Soo Pang, "Coronelismo in Northeast Brazil," in Robert Kern, ed., *The Caciques* (Albuquerque: University of New Mexico Press, 1973), pp. 65–88; Carlos N. F. Santos, "Metrópoles e Outras Cidades Brasileiras-Bem Antes de 60, Muito Depois de 80," *Espaço e Debates* 13 (1984): 103–116; Oliveira Vianna, *Instituições Políticas Brasileiras* (Rio de Janeiro: Distribuidora Record, 1974); Marcus V. Vilaça and Roberto C. de Albuquerque, *Coronel, Coroneis* (Rio de Janeiro: Tempo Brasileiro, 1965); and Francisco Weffort, *O Populismo na Política Brasileira* (São Paulo: Paz e Terra, 1980).

14. A similar point is made in a number of studies of popular political culture in Brazil. Among the most useful are Roberto Damatta, *Carnavais, Malandros e Heróis: Para uma Sociologia do Dilema Brasileiro* (Rio de Janeiro: Zahar, 1979); Renato Ortiz, *A Consciência Fragmentada* (Rio de Janeiro: Paz e Terra, 1980); Teresa Pires do Rio Caldeira, *A Política dos Outros* (São Paulo: Brasiliense, 1984); and Alba Zaluar, *A Máquina e a Revolta* (São Paulo: Brasiliense, 1985).

15. See, for example, the provocative analysis of labor relations in John D. French, *The Brazilian Workers'* ABC*: Class Conflict and Alliances in Modern São Paulo* (Chapel Hill: University of North Carolina Press, 1992).

16. In this sense, I argue that it is important to examine the political relationship between popular organizations and the state as well as issues of popular identity and culture. For a discussion of this and related issues, see Geert A. Banck, "Cultural Dilemmas Behind Strategy: Brazilian Neighborhood Movements and Catholic Discourse," *European Journal of Development Research* 2(1) (1990): 65–88; John Burdick, "Rethinking the Study of Social Movements: The Case of Christian Base Communities in Urban Brazil," in Arturo Escobar and Sonia E. Alvarez, eds., *The Making of Social Movements in Latin America* (Boulder, Colo.: Westview Press, 1992), pp. 171–184; Ruth C. L. Cardoso, "Os Movimentos Populares no Contexto da Consolidação da Democracia," in Fábio Wanderley Reis and Guillermo O'Donnell, eds., *A Democracia no Brasil: Dilemas e Perspectivas* (São Paulo: Edições Vértice, 1988), pp. 368–382; idem, "Isso é Política? Dilemas da Participação entre o Moderno e o Pós-Moderno," *Novos Estudos* 20 (1988): 74–80; idem, "Movimentos Sociais Urbanos: Balanço Crítico," in Bernardo Sorj and Maria Hermínia Tavares de Almeida, eds., *Sociedade e Política no Brasil Pós-64* (São Paulo: Brasiliense, 1983), pp. 215–239; Eunice Durham, "Movimentos Sociais: A Construção da Cidadania," *Novos Estudos* 10 (1984): 24–30; Tilman Evers, "Identity: The Hidden Side of New Social Movements in Latin America," in David Slater, ed., *New Social Movements and the State in Latin America* (Amsterdam: CEDLA, 1985), pp. 43–71; Pedro Jacobi, "Movimentos Sociais: Teoria e Prática em Questão," in Ilse Scherer-Warren and Paulo J.

Krischke, eds., *Uma Revolução no Cotidiano? Os Novos Movimentos Sociais na América Latina* (São Paulo: Brasiliense, 1987), pp. 246–275; Lúcio Kowarick, "The Pathways to Encounter: Reflections on the Social Struggle in São Paulo," in Slater, *New Social Movements*, pp. 73–94; Luiz Antônio Machado da Silva and Alícia Ziccardi, "Notas para uma Discussão Sobre Movimentos Sociais Urbanos," *Cadernos do Centro de Estudos Rurais e Urbanos* 13 (1979), pp. 79–95; Edward MacRae, "Homosexual Identities in Transitional Brazilian Politics," in Escobar and Alvarez, *Making of Social Movements*, pp. 185–203; Scott Mainwaring, "Urban Popular Movements, Identity, and Democratization in Brazil," *Comparative Political Studies* 20(2) (1987): 131–159; and Ilse Scherer-Warren, "O Carater dos Novos Movimentos Sociais," in Scherer-Warren and Krischke, *Uma Revolução no Cotidiano?* pp. 35–53.

17. Indeed, there has been a marked trend within the social sciences in general over the past two decades to develop a state-centered approach to political change. For example, see Peter Evans, Dietrich Reuschemeyer, and Theda Skocpol, eds., *Bringing the State Back In* (Cambridge: Cambridge University Press, 1985); Nora Hamilton, *The Limits of State Autonomy: Post-Revolutionary Mexico* (Princeton, N.J.: Princeton University Press, 1982); Eric Nordlinger, *On the Autonomy of the Democratic State* (Cambridge, Mass.: Harvard University Press, 1981); Theda Skocpol, *States and Social Revolutions: A Comparative Analysis of France, Russia and China* (Cambridge: Cambridge University Press, 1979); Charles Tilly, ed., *The Formation of National States in Western Europe* (Princeton, N.J.: Princeton University Press, 1975); Ellen K. Trimberger, *Revolution from Above: Military Bureaucrats and Development in Japan, Turkey, Egypt and Peru* (New Brunswick, N.J.: Transaction Books, 1978); and the exhaustive collection on democratic transitions by Guillermo O'Donnell, Philippe Schmitter, and Laurence Whitehead, eds., *Transitions from Authoritarian Rule: Prospects for Democracy* (Baltimore, Md.: Johns Hopkins University Press, 1986).

18. For a sample of recent literature on this issue, see Jean Cohen, "Strategy or Identity: New Theoretical Paradigms and Contemporary Social Movements," *Social Research* 52(4) (1985): 663–716; Charles Downs, *Revolution at the Grassroots: Community Organizations in the Portuguese Revolution* (Albany: State University of New York, 1989); Susan Eckstein, *Power and Popular Protest: Latin American Social Movements* (Berkeley: University of California Press, 1989); Escobar and Alvarez, *Making of Social Movements*; Joe Foweraker, *Making Democracy in Spain: Grass-roots Struggle in the South, 1955–1975* (Cambridge: Cambridge University Press, 1989); Foweraker and Craig, *Popular Movements*; Jane Jaquette, ed., *The Women's Movement in Latin America: Feminism and the Transition to Democracy* (Boston: Unwin Hyman, 1989); Elizabeth Jelin, *Women and Social Change in Latin America* (London: United Nations Research Institute for Social Development and Zed

Books, 1990); James Petras, "State Terror and Social Movements in Latin America," *International Journal of Politics, Culture and Society* 3(2) (1989): 179–212; Slater, *New Social Movements*; and J. Samuel Valenzuela, "Labor Movements in Transitions to Democracy," *Comparative Politics* 21 (1989): 445–472.

19. Estimates of the size of Rio's favela population are notoriously unreliable. For a long time, what was considered the definitive study of the favelas in Rio estimated that by 1967 they already housed more than 750,000 people. Popular estimates of the size of Rio's favela population range from between 2 million and 2.5 million. Recent analysis of the 1980 census, however, suggests that in 1980 the favelas of Rio housed approximately 700,000 people. For early attempts at calculating the size of Rio's favela population, see Lucien Parisse, *Favelas do Rio de Janeiro: Evolução e Sentido* (Rio de Janeiro: Centro Nacional de Pesquisas Habitacionais, 1969). For the most reliable source of information on this issue, see IPLANRIO, *Contribuição aos Dados de População das Favelas do Município do Rio de Janeiro* (Rio de Janeiro: IPLAN-RIO, 1984). For the most recent attempt to measure the population of Rio's favelas, see IPLANRIO, *Morar no Metrópole: Ensaios Sobre Habitação Popular no Rio de Janeiro* (Rio de Janeiro: IPLANRIO, 1988), pp. 40–52; and *Jornal do Brasil*, April 4, 1991, p. C6.

20. Paulo F. Cavallieri, "Favelas Cariocas: Mudanças na Infra-estrutura," in Paulo F. Cavallieri, ed., *Quatro Estudos* (Rio de Janeiro: IPLANRIO, 1986), p. 20.

21. For a discussion of illegal subdivisions in Rio, see Marcia Coutinho, "Regularização de Loteamentos: O Começo de uma Experiência no Rio de Janeiro," in Cavallieri, *Quatro Estudos*, pp. 39–54.

22. IPLANRIO, *Contribuição aos Dados*, p. 8.

23. The only favela of the size of Rocinha is Jacarezinho in Méier. The favela of Jacarezinho is estimated to house a population of 31,000 people. The next largest is Nova Brasília, also in Méier, with a population of 20,000. For information on the size of individual favelas in Rio, see ibid., p. 7.

24. It should be pointed out, however, that many of the earliest favela settlements in Rio are not represented in Table 4, as they have since been removed.

25. For urbanization, poverty, and self-help housing elsewhere in the less developed world, see Alan Gilbert and Joseph Gugler, eds., *Cities, Poverty and Development: Urbanization in the Third World* (London: Oxford University Press, 1982); and Alan Gilbert and Peter Ward, *Housing, the State and the Poor* (Cambridge: Cambridge University Press, 1985).

26. This is more true of favelas in the southern, central, and northern districts of Rio than of those located in the more distant areas of the municipality, where the provision of services is generally lacking.

27. SMDS, *Cadastro de Favelas*, vol. 3 (Rio de Janeiro: Prefeitura da Cidade do Rio de Janeiro, 1983), p. 22.

28. Ibid., p. 24.

29. The relationship among poverty, public authority, and violence in the favelas is a complex and increasingly controversial one. For a sensitive discussion of the issues in the local press, see *Jornal do Brasil*, July 29, 1990, p. C20. For an attempt to relate urban violence to general conditions of socioeconomic inequality in Rio, see Elizabeth Leeds, "The State's Use of Criminal Violence to Mask Structural Violence: Cocaine and Folk-Heroes in the Favelas of Rio de Janeiro," paper presented at the New England Council for Latin American Studies meetings (NECLAS), Wellesley College, Wellesley, Mass., 1988; and Zaluar, *Máquina e a Revolta*, pp. 132–172.

30. See, for example, *Jornal do Brasil*, September 18, 1987, p. 1.

31. See Gilda Blank, "Brás de Pina: Experiência de Urbanização de Favela," in Lícia do Prado Valladares, ed., *Habitação em Questão* (Rio de Janeiro: Zahar, 1979), p. 113; Janice Perlman, *The Myth of Marginality: Urban Poverty and Politics in Rio de Janeiro* (Berkeley: University of California Press, 1976), pp. 152–161; Lícia do Prado Valladares, *Passa-Se uma Casa: Análise do Programa de Remoção de Favelas do Rio de Janeiro* (Rio de Janeiro: Zahar, 1978), pp. 99–103; and Zaluar, *Máquina e a Revolta*, pp. 75–79.

32. A recent (unpublished) survey of Vidigal found that 57 percent of respondents between the ages of 16 and 25, 71 percent of respondents between the ages of 26 and 42, and 78 percent of respondents older than 42 had not completed primary school. It also revealed that 26 percent of respondents between the ages of 16 and 25, 13.5 percent of respondents between the ages of 26 and 42, and 6.3 percent of respondents older than 42 had completed secondary school. For a comparison with earlier data in another favela, see Perlman, *Myth of Marginality*, p. 150.

33. The neighborhood association is but one of an array of influential social, cultural, political, and religious organizations to be found in the favelas. Whatever its shortcomings, however—and there are many—the neighborhood association has been an important and ever-present link in the chain of the relationship between the population of the favelas and political elites. For a discussion of other aspects of organizational life in Rio's favelas, see Zaluar, *Máquina e a Revolta*, pp. 173–217.

NOTES TO CHAPTER 1

1. The population of the municipality of Rio increased from 274,972 in 1872 to 1,157,873 in 1920. For this and data on urban growth in other cities of Brazil, see June E. Hahner, *Poverty and Politics: The Urban Poor in Brazil, 1870–1920*, (Albuquerque: University of New Mexico Press, 1986), p. 7.

2. For an account of attempts to link housing to production during this era, see Maurício A. Abreu, "Da Habitação ao Habitat: A Questão da Habitação Popular no Rio de Janeiro e sua Evolução," *Rio de Janeiro* 2 (1986): 47–58; Eva Alterman Blay, "Dormitórios e Vilas Operárias: O Trabalhador no Espaço Urbano Brasileiro," in Lícia do Prado Valladares, ed., *Habitaçao em Questão* (Rio de Janeiro: Zahar, 1979), pp. 143–155; and Anthony Leeds and Elizabeth Leeds, *A Sociologia do Brasil Urbano* (Rio de Janeiro: Zahar, 1978), p. 189. For a discussion of working-class conditions during this period, see Sidney S. F. Solis and Marcus V. T. Ribeiro, "O Rio Onde o Sol não Brilha: Acumulação e Pobreza na Transição para o Capitalismo," *Rio de Janeiro* 1 (1986): 45–59.

3. For the political and historical context of the removals, see Hahner, *Poverty and Politics*, pp. 160–165; Jeffrey Needell, *A Tropical Belle Epoque: Elite Culture and Society in Turn-of-the-Century Rio de Janeiro* (Cambridge: Cambridge University Press, 1987), pp. 33–51; Oswaldo P. Rocha, "A Era das Demolições: Cidade do Rio de Janeiro: 1870–1920," master's thesis, Instituto de Ciências Humanas e Filosofia, Níteroi, Brazil, 1982; and Victor V. Valla, *Educação e Favela: Política para as Favelas do Rio de Janeiro* (Rio de Janeiro: Zahar, 1986), pp. 30–31.

4. The first favelas to be established in Rio were those of Providência and Santo Antônio in 1897. These favelas were also among the first to be removed following the outbreak of a flu epidemic in 1918. See Lucien Parisse, *Favelas do Rio de Janeiro: Evolução e Sentido* (Rio de Janeiro: Centro Nacional de Pesquisas Habitacionais), p. 13.

5. Douglas H. Graham and Sérgio Buarque de Hollanda Filho, *Migrações Internas no Brasil: 1872–1970* (São Paulo: IPE/USP, 1984), pp. 91–93; and Victor V. Valla, *A Penetração Norte-Americano na Economia Brasileira, 1898–1928* (Rio de Janeiro: Livro Tecnico S/A, 1979), p. 137.

6. *Código de Obras*, 1937, articles 347 and 349.

7. It was also suggested that the state might restrict the entry of migrants to the city by persuading them to return to their places of origin. See, for example, Parisse, *Favelas do Rio de Janeiro*, pp. 66–67.

8. Leeds and Leeds, *Sociologia do Brasil Urbano*, pp. 191–198; Parisse, *Favelas do Rio de Janeiro*, pp. 66–77; and Valla, *Educação e Favela*, pp. 34–42.

9. The advent of democratic politics witnessed an end, for the time being, to systematic attempts to remove all favelas from Rio. It did not, however, put a stop to the removal of individual favelas. Nor did it do away with the idea that the favelas should ultimately be torn down.

10. For the changing nature of state policy toward the urban poor elsewhere in Latin America, see David Collier, *Squatters and Oligarchs: Authoritarian Rule and Policy Change in Peru* (Baltimore, Md.: Johns Hopkins University Press, 1976), pp. 124–125; Wayne Cornelius, *Politics and the Migrant Poor in Mexico City* (Stanford, Calif.: Stanford University Press, 1975), p. 203; and

Talton Ray, *The Politics of the Barrios of Venezuela* (Berkeley: University of California Press, 1969), pp. 31–33.

11. The fear that the urban poor represent a potentially revolutionary force was by no means specific to Brazil. See, for example, Frantz Fanon, *The Wretched of the Earth* (London: MacGibbon and Kee, 1965).

12. The Fundação Leão XIII and the Cruzada São Sebastião were agencies administered by the Catholic church in Rio. SERFHA, on the other hand, was a creation of the federal government. For a discussion of the mandate and history of these three institutions, see Leeds and Leeds, *Sociologia do Brasil Urbano*, pp. 198–214; and Valla, *Educação e Favela*, pp. 44–55.

13. The Fundação Leão XIII was created by presidential decree as an independent body that was to be administered by the Catholic church in Rio. In 1962 Lacerda subordinated it to the Secretaria de Serviços Sociais of the recently created state of Guanabara. See Leeds and Leeds, *Sociologia do Brasil Urbano*, pp. 214–215.

14. Ibid., p. 213.

15. Two of the more interesting descriptions of favela politics during this era can be found in Luis Antônio Machado da Silva, "A Política na Favela," *Cadernos Brasileiros* 9(41) (1967): 35–47; and Carlos A. Medina, *A Favela e o Demagogo* (São Paulo: Impressa Livre, 1964).

16. For a discussion of the removal process in Rio and of the political context in which it occurred, see Sérgio A. Azevedo and Luis A. G. Andrade, *Habitação e Poder: Da Fundação da Casa Popular ao Banco Nacional da Habitação* (Rio de Janeiro: Zahar, 1981); Leeds and Leeds, *Sociologia do Brasil Urbano*, pp. 214–247; Janice Perlman, *The Myth of Marginality: Urban Poverty and Politics in Rio de Janeiro* (Berkeley: University of California Press, 1976), pp. 195–241; Rio de Janeiro, "Á Margem, Cresce a Grande Cidade: Favela," *Revista do Tribunal de Contas do Município do Rio de Janeiro* 1 (1981): 53–60; Valla, *Educação e Favela*, pp. 85–111; and Lícia do Prado Valladares, *Passa-Se uma Casa: Análise do Programa de Remoção de Favelas do Rio de Janeiro* (Rio de Janeiro: Zahar, 1978).

17. Leeds and Leeds, *Sociologia do Brasil Urbano*, p. 230; and Valla, *Educação e Favela*, p. 89.

18. The forced relocation of slum dwellers to expensive and largely inappropriate public-housing projects on the periphery has been a constant theme in Latin American urban history. For example, see Collier, *Squatters and Oligarchs*, pp. 28–29; Cornelius, *Politics and the Migrant Poor*, p. 208; and Ray, *Politics of the Barrios*, p. 32.

19. CODESCO was the fruit of a series of initiatives funded by USAID that looked to promote self-help projects in the favelas. See Valla, *Educação e Favela*, pp. 94–97.

20. Lacerda failed in his bid for reelection as governor, some say as a result of his active role in the removal of favelas in Rio. See ibid., pp. 94–95.

21. Gilda Blank, "Brás de Pina: Experiência de Urbanização de Favela," in Valladares, *Habitação em Questão*, pp. 93–124; and Carlos N. F. Santos, "Some Considerations About the Possibilities of Squatter Settlements Redevelopment Plans: The Case of Brás de Pina," master's thesis, MIT, Cambridge, Mass., 1971.

22. Decreto "N" 870 of June 15, 1967, and Decreto "E" 3,330 of November 3, 1969.

23. There is some debate over whether state intervention into the affairs of favela neighborhood associations effectively stifled popular resistance. For a discussion of this issue, see Valladares, *Passa-Se uma Casa*, pp. 112–118. For a discussion of state control of neighborhood associations elsewhere in Latin America, see Collier, *Squatters and Oligarchs*, p. 61; Ray, *Politics of the Barrios*, p. 92; and Alfred Stepan, *The State and Society: Peru in Comparative Perspective* (Princeton, N.J.: Princeton University Press, 1978), pp. 158–189.

24. While 65 percent of all favela removals took place between 1968 and 1974, between 1970 and 1974 the total number of favelas in Rio actually increased by 74 percent. See Valladares, *Passa-Se uma Casa*, p. 44.

25. For details of the impact of relocation, see IPLANRIO, *Morar na Metrópole: Ensaios Sobre Habitação Popular no Rio de Janeiro* (Rio de Janeiro: IPLANRIO, 1988), pp. 9–32; Perlman, *Myth of Marginality*, pp. 211–223; Barbara Rush, "From Favela to Conjunto: The Experience of Squatters Removed to Low-Cost Housing in Rio de Janeiro, Brazil," honors thesis, Harvard College, Cambridge, Mass., 1974; and Valladares, *Passa-Se uma Casa*, pp. 63–104.

26. It should be pointed out that elections for state deputy, federal deputy, and senator were held throughout the authoritarian era, so the relationship between the population of the favelas and political elites was never completely closed off.

27. Eli Diniz, *Voto e Máquina Política: Clientelismo e Patronagem no Rio de Janeiro* (Rio de Janeiro: Paz e Terra, 1982), pp. 49–64.

28. For the rise of the MDB, see Eli Diniz, "Máquinas Políticas e Oposição: O MDB no Rio de Janeiro," *Dados* 23(3) (1980): 335–357; and Diniz, *Voto e Máquina Política*, pp. 90–95.

29. The state of Guanabara merged with the state of Rio de Janeiro in 1975.

30. Diniz, *Voto e Máquina Política*, pp. 96–125.

31. FAFEG became the Federação de Associações de Favelas do Estado do Rio de Janeiro (FAFERJ) with the fusion of the states of Guanabara and Rio de Janeiro in 1975.

32. It was with an eye to these same elections that the federal government introduced a program known as Projeto Rio to upgrade a large area of favela housing in an area of the city known as Maré. For an analysis of this program, see Valla, *Educação e Favela*, p. 141.

33. In this sense there are distinct parallels between the problems encountered by the SMDS and SERFHA under Lacerda.

34. Valla, *Educação e Favela*, pp. 152–153.

35. For a discussion of the bureaucratic, political, and financial problems that plagued the SMDS, see Tema Pechman, "A Política de Intervenção em Áreas Faveladas: O Município do Rio de Janeiro," paper presented at the Associação Nacional de Pós-Graduação e Pesquisa em Ciências Sociais meetings (ANPOCS), Friburgo, Brazil, 1982.

36. The comissões de luz were established in the early 1960s to regularize the provision of electricity to the favelas. They subsequently became a mechanism for economic and political exploitation.

37. The program was originally designed to mobilize political support for the PDS in Rio, and it was only the constant vigilance of the managerial staff that kept interference from political interests to a minimum. Having said this, one of the technicians involved with the project informed me that a considerable amount of the money allocated to the program by the federal government found its way into the pockets of PDS politicians by the time of the elections in 1982. Furthermore, the president of LIGHT was himself a candidate for the PDS nomination for governor, and the principal director of the program was a PDS candidate for state deputy. For an excellent discussion of political, social, and technical aspects of the program in Rio, see Olga Bronstein, "De Cima para Baixo ou de Baixo para Cima? Considerações em Torno da Oferta de um Serviço Público nas Favelas do Rio de Janeiro," paper presented at the Associação Nacional de Pós-Graduação e Pesquisa em Ciências Sociais meetings (ANPOCS), Friburgo, Brazil, 1982.

38. Diniz, *Voto e Máquina Política*, pp. 139–154.

39. For an analysis of the attitudes of leaders of individual neighborhood associations toward the dissident federation and FAFERJ in 1980, see Eli Diniz, "Favela: Associativismo e Participação Social," in Renato R. Boschi, ed., *Movimentos Coletivos no Brasil Urbano* (Rio de Janeiro: Zahar, 1982), pp. 53–60.

40. By 1986 there were an estimated 80,000 grass-roots church organizations in Brazil. The impact of these organizations varies substantially on a regional level, however, according to the specific nature of each bishopric. The bishopric of Rio de Janeiro is one of the more conservative in Brazil. Therefore, changes in the orientation of the church had less of an impact in Rio than in other areas. For a discussion of this and related issues, see Frances O'Gorman, *Base Communities in Brazil* (Rio de Janeiro: Francisco Alves, 1983).

41. In recognition of the fact that the MDB was associated with the opposition and the PDS with the military, new parties were prohibited from adopting the titles of either party that participated in the biparty system. Of course, this was designed primarily to benefit the government party. The other parties that emerged as a result of the reforms were the PTB, the Partido dos Trabalhadores (PT), and the Partido Democrático Trabalhista (PDT).

42. *Jornal do Brasil*, April 26, 1982, p. 5.

43. The PDT as a party came into being only because Brizola lost the juridical battle for control of the PTB symbol.

44. For a discussion of the demise of the MDB in Rio, see Eli Diniz, "Voto e Realinhamento Eleitoral no Rio de Janeiro," *C and P* 2(1–2) (1984): 77–99.

45. See, for example, comments made in defeat by the PMDB candidate Teixeira regarding the efficacy of clientelism as a mechanism of political mobilization (*Jornal do Brasil*, November 19, 1982, p. 4).

46. For an overview of the PDT's programs in the favelas of Rio, see Paulo F. Cavallieri, "Favelas Cariocas: Mudanças na Infra-estrutura," in Paulo F. Cavallieri, ed., *Quatro Estudos* (Rio de Janeiro: IPLANRIO, 1986), pp. 25–34; and SECPLAN, *Bairros Populares e Favelas* (Rio de Janeiro: SECPLAN, 1985).

47. The logic of this strategy was explained to me by one of the project coordinators of the SMDS.

48. *Jornal do Brasil*, July 27, 1986, p. 18.

49. Interview with author, February 24, 1986.

50. Braga was one of the politicians who fled the ranks of the PMDB following the return of the Chaguistas in 1979.

51. FAMERJ comprised neighborhood associations from middle-class areas of the city of Rio de Janeiro and neighborhood associations from other municipalities in the state.

52. Interview with author, May 30, 1986.

NOTES TO CHAPTER 2

1. Of the 427 illegal subdivisions recorded in the municipality in 1984, almost all (81 percent) were located in Bangu, Campo Grande, and Santa Cruz.

2. IPLANRIO, *Contribuição aos Dados de População das Favelas do Município do Rio de Janeiro* (Rio de Janeiro: IPLANRIO, 1984), p. 7.

3. Guida Nunes, *Rio: Metrópole de 300 Favelas* (Rio de Janeiro: Vozes, 1978), p. 126.

4. See Eli Diniz, *Voto e Máquina Política: Clientelismo e Patronagem no Rio de Janeiro* (Rio de Janeiro: Paz e Terra, 1982), pp. 104–118; and *Jornal do Brasil*, October 15, 1986, p. C13.

5. The terms "Chaguismo" and "Brizolismo" are popularly used to describe a style of politics associated with certain political leaders.

6. The information in this section was drawn from extensive conversations with the participants of the favela movement in Zona Oeste and from interviews with Father John Klebin in November 1989 and August 1991.

7. Interview with author, May 5, 1986.

8. On the eve of the elections in 1986 the PDT was also in the process of granting tenure rights to sixteen favelas in the region.

9. I found official estimates of the population of Vila Brasil to be highly unreliable. For example, in 1979 the Secretaria Municipal de Planejamento estimated there to be 3,000 people living in 563 houses in Vila Brasil. Yet in the same year, the Secretaria Municipal de Desenvolvimento Social (SMDS) estimated that there were 3,500 people in only 100 houses!

10. The breakdown of the occupational structure of the favela of Vila Brasil was taken from a follow-up survey conducted immediately prior to the presidential elections in 1989.

11. In this sense, I tend to disagree with much of the recent literature on low-income settlements in Latin America that questions the notion of "community" among the urban poor. At least in Rio, the fact that an individual lives in a favela and is, therefore, a *favelado* (a "slum dweller") is an important aspect of his or her self-concept and social identity. For similar observations in the context of Lima, Peru, see Carol Graham, "The APRA Government and the Urban Poor: The PAIT Programme in Lima's Pueblos Jóvenes," *Journal of Latin American Studies* 23 (1991): 93.

12. The samba block has since stopped functioning in Vila Brasil.

13. The observation that local-level political brokers in Latin America tend to monopolize the decision-making process is a common one. See, for example, Wayne Cornelius, *Politics and the Migrant Poor in Mexico City* (Stanford, Calif.: Stanford University Press, 1975), p. 153; Susan Eckstein, *The Poverty of Revolution: The State and the Urban Poor in Mexico* (Princeton, N.J.: Princeton University Press, 1977), p. 83; and Susan Stokes, "Politics and Latin America's Urban Poor: Reflections from a Lima Shantytown," *Latin American Research Review* 26(2) (1991): 83.

14. The president informed me with pride that during the last few years of his tenure as a stevedore he spent most of his time selling contraband while paying someone else to do his "official" work. Many of the contacts he established during this time proved to be invaluable when he took over the presidency of the neighborhood association in Vila Brasil.

15. In this sense, the president of Vila Brasil is a master in the art of deception since his obsequiousness in the presence of politicians and administrators is pure theater. For a discussion of this and related issues, see Cornelius, *Politics and the Migrant Poor*, p. 185; and James C. Scott, *Weapons of the Weak* (New Haven, Conn.: Yale University Press, 1985).

16. This transaction was witnessed in horror and amazement by representatives from the Pastoral de Favelas.

17. Although the electoral district of which Vila Brasil is a part covers an area that is much larger than the favela, candidates who invest money can check to see whether they received a disproportionate number of votes in the area. Candidates can, therefore, obtain a rough idea of the efficacy of a particular transaction and the ability of a particular president or political broker to deliver the vote.

18. One day the president took me over to see one of two plots of land that he had bought outside the favela. It was full of building materials that he told me had been sent to him by, among others, one Leonel Brizola.

19. In this sense, the president of Vila Brasil differs from political leaders to be found elsewhere in Latin America in that he expresses no affinity with local political elites. For an alternative view of the relationship between local leaders and elites in Latin America, see Cornelius, *Politics and the Migrant Poor*, pp. 159–160; Eckstein, *Poverty of Revolution*, p. 99; Talton Ray, *The Politics of the Barrios of Venezuela* (Berkeley: University of California Press, 1969), pp. 61–63; and Stokes, "Politics and Latin America's Urban Poor," 87.

20. This strategy is popularly known as *jogo de cintura*, literally, making the best of a situation.

21. According to the president, the two politicians were elected because of the peculiarities of the electoral legislation that year. Voters were obliged to choose candidates from a single party. Those who chose Brizola for governor were then confronted with a list of virtual unknowns in the elections for other offices. In the absence of alternative criteria, these same voters opted for names they were at least familiar with.

22. Neither candidate from Zona Oeste was reelected in 1986 when there were no such restrictions on voting behavior.

23. Most analyses of neighborhood associations and other such organizations in Latin America claim that local leaders are largely in it for their own gain. This was clearly not the case in Vila Brasil. For the view that leaders are in it for their own gain, see Cornelius, *Politics and the Migrant Poor*, p. 143; and Eckstein, *Poverty of Revolution*, p. 91.

24. Leite received only 8.6 percent of the vote in the elections for mayor in Rio in 1985, third to Braga of the PDT with 39.5 percent, and Roberto Medina of the Partido da Frente Liberal (PFL) with 17.1 percent.

25. For a similar strategy, see Judith Hellman's discussion of Pedro Gallardo in Hellman, "The Role of Ideology in Peasant Politics: Peasant Mobilization and Demobilization in the Laguna Region," *Journal of Interamerican Studies and World Affairs* 25(1) (1983): 12–16.

26. So much so that at one regional FAFERJ meeting the leadership asked the president of Vila Brasil to act out his role so that others could identify the difference between "good" politics and "bad" politics!

27. The president of Vila Brasil's relationship with FAFERJ and the fact that his advice was solicited by other leaders in the region contradicts the widely held belief that clientelism necessarily precludes communication and collaboration among the urban poor. See, for example, Eckstein, *Poverty of Revolution*, p. 89.

NOTES TO CHAPTER 3

1. Lícia do Prado Valladares, *Passa-Se uma Casa: Análise do Programa de Remoção de Favelas do Rio de Janeiro* (Rio de Janeiro: Zahar, 1978), p. 31.
2. Anthony Leeds and Elizabeth Leeds, *A Sociologia do Brasil Urbano* (Rio de Janeiro: Zahar, 1978), p. 220; and Guida Nunes, *Rio: Metrópole de 300 Favelas* (Rio de Janeiro: Vozes, 1978), p. 49.
3. Rio de Janeiro, "Á Margem, Cresce a Grande Cidade: Favela," *Revista do Tribunal de Contas do Município do Rio de Janeiro* 1 (1981): 53–60.
4. SECPLAN, *Bairros Populares e Favelas* (Rio de Janeiro; SECPLAN, 1985).
5. For an analysis of the strength of the Chaguista vote in the favelas and in other areas of Zona Sul, see Eli Diniz, *Voto e Máquina Política: Clientelismo e Patronagem no Rio de Janeiro* (Rio de Janeiro: Paz e Terra, 1982), p. 83.
6. During the dictatorship the Catholic church played a critical role in assisting individual favelas and helping reorganize the favela movement. Since then, however, it has been forced to compete for hearts and minds with neighborhood associations, political parties, women's groups, and other religious denominations. Thus, even in Vidigal, where the church's influence has been particularly strong, there has been a marked decline in attendance at local Pastoral meetings and a distancing of the leadership of the neighborhood association from the church. Furthermore, while grateful for all that the church has done, the leadership of the neighborhood association understands that the church has its own agenda and its own political interests. For a discussion of this and related issues, see Geert A. Banck, "Cultural Dilemmas Behind Strategy: Brazilian Neighborhood Movements and Catholic Discourse," *European Journal of Development Research* 2(1) (1990): 65–88; and John Burdick, "Rethinking the Study of Social Movements: The Case of Christian Base Communities in Urban Brazil," in Arturo Escobar and Sonia E. Alvarez, eds., *The Making of Social Movements in Latin America* (Boulder, Colo.: Westview Press, 1992), pp. 171–184.
7. As with Vila Brasil, official estimates of the population of Vidigal tend to be highly unreliable. In 1979 the Secretaria Municipal de Planejamento calculated there to be 26,425 inhabitants in approximately 5,000 dwellings. And yet, in the same year the SMDS reported there to be 12,000 in 2,400 dwellings!
8. Depending on its location, a simple house can be bought for as little as three thousand dollars in Vidigal. And rental accommodation, though hard to come by, is also available if the price is right.
9. The breakdown of occupations in Vidigal was taken from a survey of political attitudes in the favela immediately prior to the .presidential elections in 1989.
10. For example, during the presidency of José Sarney the federal government

issued free milk tokens to many favela communities in Rio. In Vidigal this program was administered by the neighborhood association. The neighborhood association registered families whose head of household earned one minimum salary or less. These families were then told to turn up at the first neighborhood association meeting of every month to receive their allocation of tokens.

11. Interview with author, November 11, 1986.
12. For a journalistic account of the events surrounding the eviction attempt, see Guida Nunes, *Favela: Resistência pelo Direito de Viver* (Petrópolis, Brazil: Vozes, 1980), pp. 124–135.
13. *Jornal do Brasil*, January 4, 1978, p. 26.
14. *Jornal do Brasil*, October 28, 1977, p. 8.
15. *O Globo*, January 10, 1978, p. 15.
16. Rio de Janeiro, "Margem," 53–60; and Valladares, *Passa-Se uma Casa*, pp. 29–30.
17. Interview with author, October 30, 1986.
18. The significance of the events in Vidigal for the local church was recognized when Pope John Paul II paid a visit to Vidigal during his brief stay in Brazil in 1980.
19. For a similar discussion of different forms of interest representation among the urban poor in Peru, see Susan Stokes, "Politics and Latin America's Urban Poor: Reflections from a Lima Shantytown," *Latin American Research Review* 26(2) (1991): 81–82.
20. Interview with author, November 12, 1986.
21. Interview with author, November 12, 1986.
22. For a similar distinction between the more immediate and material kinds of demands and the more political and universal kinds of demands made by the urban poor, see Stokes, "Politics and Latin America's Urban Poor," 83–84.
23. Interview with author, November 12, 1986.
24. This victory was to be his last, however.
25. Such politicians were commonly referred to as *autênticos*.
26. Diniz, *Voto e Máquina Política*, pp. 78–81.
27. *Jornal do Brasil*, January 7, 1980, p. 3.
28. For a discussion of the Pope's visit, see *Jornal do Brasil*, May 6, 1983, p. 7. For a discussion of the tendency for popular organizations and the state to compete for the political capital associated with public works, see Ruth C. L. Cardoso, "Os Movimentos Populares no Contexto da Consolidação da Democracia," in Fábio Wanderley Reis and Guillermo O'Donnell, eds., *A Democracia no Brasil: Dilemas e Perspectivas* (São Paulo: Edições Vértice, 1988), p. 376.
29. For a discussion of similar issues with regard to APRA and the Programa de

Apoyo de Ingreso Temporal (PAIT) in Peru, see Carol Graham, "The APRA Government and the Urban Poor: The PAIT Programme in Lima's Pueblos Jóvenes," *Journal of Latin American Studies* 23 (1991): 117.

30. A good example of this is provided by President José Sarney's March 1986 anti-inflation package, otherwise known as the Plano Cruzado. The package provoked a good deal of debate among the leadership of the neighborhood association in Vidigal. And while most of the directors of the neighborhood association were critical of the wage freeze, arguing that wages had been frozen at a particularly low level, they were generally supportive of the price freeze in that it proved initially successful in reducing inflation from its previous high of about 15 percent per month. They were, therefore, singularly unimpressed and somewhat insulted by Brizola's crude televised assault on the program.

31. Interview with author, November 12, 1986.

32. Interview with author, November 12, 1986.

33. In point of fact, the group of individuals that led the favela's resistance against removal in 1977 and 1978 was much the same group that formed the first neighborhood association in Vidigal ten years earlier.

34. For example, until it was discontinued in 1990, two former presidents of the neighborhood association and militants within the PMDB were employed full-time by President Sarney's Secretaria Especial de Ação Comunitária (SEAC), an agency that was specifically designed to build support among the urban poor. It has also been fairly common for those who sympathize with the PDT to work as advisers to government projects in the favelas.

35. One female director affiliated with the PT told me she felt that the neighborhood association was taking too passive a stance vis-à-vis the PDT precisely because of the large number of PDT supporters among the directorate.

36. Many of those who are involved in the samba block and the soccer club are also directors of the neighborhood association, so there is no great disparity between the different organizations' respective philosophies.

37. It seems as though each time I return to the favela of Vidigal these days I am told of the death of a whole new generation of drug dealers.

38. A functionary of IPLANRIO, the municipal planning agency, told me of her difficulties in persuading young men to enroll in a scheme to install workshops in the favelas. She discovered that the wages offered by the scheme could not compete with the wages to be earned as a lookout for the gangs.

39. The fact that young men who ten years ago would never have considered joining the drug gang were now volunteering their services was an observation made by my teenaged friends in the favela on many occasions.

NOTES TO CHAPTER 4

1. As a favela, the one thing that the community lacked, of course, was the right of legal tenure. The president considered this to be outside of the realm of possibility for local-level clientelist politics, however.

2. The movement of politicians from one party to another is common in Brazil. For example, in 1982 the PDT in Rio elected twenty-four representatives to the State Assembly. By July of 1986, however, it had increased its share to thirty-three, despite losing three of those it had elected in 1982. Those who defected to the PDT came from a variety of different parties but primarily from those of the Right. Thus, between 1982 and 1986 the PDT welcomed two politicians from the Partido Trabalhista Brasileiro (PTB), five from the PMDB, and five from the Partido Democrático Social (PDS). The political credentials of these defectors were never at issue; what was important was the fact that they occupied a seat in the house and the fact that they commanded a winning margin of votes in their respective political constituencies.

3. It is important to point out that Oswaldo was financing his "campaign expenses" out of his own pocket. So unlike Leite before him, he was not siphoning off public resources.

4. Of course, it was somewhat less of a coincidence that the president of the neighborhood association worked with candidates from the PMDB in 1982 and 1986, considering that the PMDB has in the past provided a home to more than its fair share of politicians looking to make such a deal.

5. All except Oswaldo, however, gave the president small amounts of money to pay for the distribution of campaign literature. The president allocated his time and energy accordingly.

6. For a similar strategy by APRA in Peru, see Carol Graham, "The APRA Government and the Urban Poor: The PAIT Programme in Lima's Pueblos Jóvenes," *Journal of Latin American Studies* 23 (1991): 115.

7. Interestingly enough, the only ones at the meeting to defend the candidate's position were representatives of FAFERJ's central executive!

8. These candidates were Wellington Moreira Franco (PMDB) for governor, Pedro Mello (Partido Liberal, PL) for federal deputy, and Marcelino D'Almeida (PL) for state deputy.

9. For a discussion of the problem of the "free rider" for collective action, see Mancur Olson, *The Logic of Collective Action* (Cambridge, Mass.: Harvard University Press, 1971).

10. Interview with author, September 24, 1986.

11. Interview with author, September 24, 1986.

12. Interview with author, September 24, 1986.

13. Interview with author, September 24, 1986.

14. Interview with author, October 30, 1986.

15. The original neighborhood association building had two storys. An extra story has since been added on but is little more than a parapet.

16. Having said this, it is important not to overestimate the general awareness of, or interest in, this aspect of the November elections. The neighborhood association scheduled a slide show and debate on the new constitution for a Saturday three weeks prior to the election, and even provided free beer (usually incentive enough). As fate would have it, it turned out to be a steaming hot October day when everyone bar the directorate was lured away by that other great carioca passion, the beach.

17. Interview with author, November 12, 1986.

18. That so many of Brizola's former secretaries ran for public office in 1986 is indicative of the highly centralized style of the PDT. The success of many of them is testimony to the popularity of the administration's programs, especially in the poorer neighborhoods of the city.

19. The land was to be handed over to the neighborhood association as communal property. It was up to the neighborhood association, therefore, to decide who got what and where.

20. Interview with author, November 12, 1986.

21. In retrospect, the president of the neighborhood association was well advised to turn down the offer, given that SEAC was abruptly discontinued when Fernando Collor took office as president of Brazil in 1990.

NOTES TO CHAPTER 5

1. The elections were the first for governor to include the votes of illiterates and the first for governor since the creation of the biparty system in 1965 without severe restrictions on political-party organization. The elections were also relatively free of voting restrictions in that, unlike 1982, there was no voto vinculado.

2. Until the end of February the PDT's chances of making inroads into other parts of the country looked good. The situation changed, however, with the announcement of the Plano Cruzado, a package of measures designed to control inflation and revitalize the economy via strict wage and price control. The Plano Cruzado met with such a wave of popular support that it stifled dissent from within the governing alliance and forced the political opposition onto the defensive.

3. Sarney had only recently assumed the presidency following the untimely death of Tancredo Neves. A native of the state of Maranhão, Sarney began his political career with the Partido Social Democrático (PSD), moved to the União Democrática Nacional (UDN), and formed part of a political front known as the Frente Parlamentar Nacionalista (FPN) led, ironically, by Brizola. In the wake of the coup in 1964 and the creation of a biparty system, Sarney joined the ranks of Aliança Renovadora Nacional (ARENA). Once in ARENA he was elected to the Senate, with full support of the military, in 1970 and again in 1978. In 1979 he assumed the presidency of ARENA at the invitation of then-president Figueiredo. In 1980 he became the president of the newly created Partido Democrático Social (PDS), a position he held until May 1984. Following the nomination of ex-governor of São Paulo Paulo Maluf as the party's presidential candidate, Sarney joined the swelling ranks of PDS politicians who abandoned ship in favor of Neves. Sarney's insertion as Neves's running mate in the presidential election in 1985 was an important factor in securing the success of the alliance against the military. That someone so closely associated with the military should become president as a result of a victory sustained primarily by the party of opposition, the Partido do Movimento Democrático Brasileiro (PMDB), is one of the beautiful ironies of Brazilian politics.

4. The alliance brought together the following parties: the PMDB, the PFL, the PCB, the PTB, the PCdoB, the Partido Trabalhista Renovador (PTR), the Partido Trabalhista Nacional (PTN), the Partido Democrático Cristão (PDC), the Partido da Mobilização Nacional (PMN), the Partido Municipalista Comunitário (PMC), the Partido do Povo Brasileiro (PPB), and the Partido Comunitário Nacional (PCN).

5. The PT's candidate for governor in 1986 reflected the character of the party in Rio. A former guerilla and now successful author, Fernando Gabeira's campaign focused more on racial, ecological, and sexual issues than on traditional working-class demands.

6. For further details, see the Appendix.

7. Leite's popularity in the favela is all the more impressive if one considers that three respondents mistakenly named Leite as their candidate of choice for a seat in the State Assembly (an error that no doubt would have been corrected on seeing the candidate's name in its correct position on the ballot sheet) and that the second most popular candidate in Vila Brasil, Ronaldo Rios of the PDC, was cited by a mere 4 percent of all those who were interviewed.

8. Voters in 1986 were required to choose one candidate for governor, one candidate for federal deputy, one candidate for state deputy, and two candidates for senator.

9. The next most popular candidate, also from the APD, was cited by a meager 3 percent of respondents to the survey.

10. It is interesting that this sexual imbalance is less noticeable among supporters of Leite, in that nearly 44 percent of those who said they were going

to vote for the ex-Chaguista were men. By way of contrast, Leite's electorate in Vila Brasil—at least in this election—was disproportionately young, educated, and of longer standing in the community!

11. It should be obvious from these figures that not all Leite voters were Oswaldo voters, or vice versa.

12. This does not mean that the two candidates were not interested in pushing their names in the favela. Vasconcellos, if you remember, kept his name alive by supplying generous rounds of food and drink to the soccer club for its many excursions. The neighborhood association was well aware that there was a reason for Vasconcellos's generosity that went beyond the realm of friendship. Vasconcellos never demanded anything in return, however. If his gifts to the favela generated good will toward his candidacy, fine. If they did not, too bad.

13. This is the basis of most explanations of the relationship between Brizola and the population of the favelas.

14. Approximately 40 percent of respondents who had decided on a candidate or party of their choice could give no specific reason for that choice. This finding was consistent for the elections for governor, senator, federal deputy, and state deputy.

15. The second most popular response (22 percent) cited the candidate's good looks and cheery disposition. It is interesting to note that most of those who said they were following the president's instructions were women. It would appear, therefore, that the president had more direct influence among the female population of the favela than among the male population.

NOTES TO THE APPENDIX

1. It was particularly important and informative in this regard to check the president's stories with other residents of Vila Brasil, with representatives of the Pastoral de Favelas and FAFERJ who were often present at these meetings, and with state functionaries that had administered government programs in Vila Brasil and Zona Oeste.

2. This was particularly important in Vidigal, where one of my research assistants, who was also a good friend, was the girlfriend of one of the local traficantes.

3. Education and income were not controlled for because of the relative homogeneity of the population of the two favelas with regard to these two variables.

Bibliography

Abreu, Maurício A. "Da Habitação ao Habitat: A Questão da Habitação Popular no Rio de Janeiro e sua Evolução." *Rio de Janeiro* 2 (1986): 47–58.

Alvarez, Sonia E. *Engendering Democracy in Brazil.* Princeton, N.J.: Princeton University Press, 1990.

Azevedo, Sérgio A., and Luis A. G. Andrade. *Habitação e Poder: Da Fundação da Casa Popular ao Banco Nacional da Habitação.* Rio de Janeiro: Zahar, 1981.

Baer, Werner, Isaac Kerstenetsky, and Anibal Villela. "The Changing Role of the State in the Brazilian Economy." *World Development* 1 (1973): 23–34.

Banck, Geert A. "Cultural Dilemmas Behind Strategy: Brazilian Neighborhood Movements and Catholic Discourse." *European Journal of Development Research* 2(1) (1990): 65–88.

———. "Poverty, Politics and the Shaping of Urban Space: A Brazilian Example." *International Journal of Urban and Regional Research* 10(4) (1986): 522–540.

Blank, Gilda. "Brás de Pina: Experiência de Urbanização de Favela." In Lícia do Prado Valladares, ed., *Habitação em Questão*, pp. 93–124. Rio de Janeiro: Zahar, 1979.

Blay, Eva Alterman. "Dormitórios e Vilas Operárias: O Trabalhador no Espaço Urbano Brasileiro." In Lícia do Prado Valladares, ed., *Habitação em Questão*, pp. 143–155. Rio de Janeiro: Zahar, 1979.

Borja, Jordi. *Movimentos Sociales Urbanos.* Buenos Aires: Ediçiones SIAP, 1975.

Boschi, Renato R. *A Arte da Associação, Política de Base e Democracia no Brasil.* São Paulo: Edições Vértice, 1987.

Bronstein, Olga. "De Cima para Baixo ou de Baixo para Cima? Considerações em Torno da Oferta de um Serviço Público nas Favelas do Rio de Janeiro." Paper presented at the Associação Nacional de Pós-Graduação e Pesquisa em Ciências Sociais meetings (ANPOCS), Friburgo, Brazil, 1982.

Burdick, John. "Rethinking the Study of Social Movements: The Case of Christian Base Communities in Urban Brazil." In Arturo Escobar and Sonia E. Alvarez, eds., *The Making of Social Movements in Latin America*, pp. 171–184. Boulder, Colo.: Westview Press, 1992.

Camargo, Aspásia, and **Eli Diniz,** eds. *Continuidade e Mudança no Brasil da Nova República.* Rio de Janeiro: Edições Vértice and IUPERJ, 1989.

Cammack, Paul. "Clientelism and Military Government in Brazil." In Christopher Clapham, ed., *Private Patronage and Public Power*, pp. 53–75. New York: St. Martin's Press, 1982.

Campello de Souza, Maria do Carmo. *Estado e Partidos Políticos no Brasil (1930 a 1964).* São Paulo: Alfa-Ômega, 1976.

Cardoso, Fernando Henrique. *Empresário Industrial e Desenvolvimento Econômico no Brasil.* São Paulo: Difel, 1964.

Cardoso, Ruth C. L. "Isso é Política? Dilemas da Participação entre o Moderno e o Pós-Moderno." *Novos Estudos* 20 (1988): 74–80.

———. "Os Movimentos Populares no Contexto da Consolidação da Democracia." In Fábio Wanderley Reis and Guillermo O'Donnell, eds., *A Democracia no Brasil: Dilemas e Perspectivas*, pp. 368–382. São Paulo: Edições Vértice, 1988.

———. "Movimentos Sociais Urbanos: Balanço Crítico." In Bernardo Sorj and Maria Hermínia Tavares de Almeida, eds., *Sociedade e Política no Brasil Pós-64*, pp. 215–239. São Paulo: Brasiliense, 1983.

Castells, Manuel. *City, Class and Power.* London: Macmillan, 1978.

———. *The Urban Question.* London: Edward Arnold, 1977.

Cavallieri, Paulo F. "Favelas Cariocas: Mudanças na Infra-estrutura." In Paulo F. Cavallieri, ed., *Quatro Estudos*, pp. 19–38. Rio de Janeiro: IPLANRIO, 1986.

Cohen, Jean. "Strategy or Identity: New Theoretical Paradigms and Contemporary Social Movements." *Social Research* 52(4) (1985): 663–716.

Cohen, Youssef. *The Manipulation of Consent.* Pittsburgh, Pa.: University of Pittsburgh Press, 1989.

Collier, David. *Squatters and Oligarchs: Authoritarian Rule and Policy Change in Peru.* Baltimore, Md.: Johns Hopkins University Press, 1976.

Collier, Ruth B. "Popular Sector Incorporation and Political Supremacy: Regime Evolution in Brazil and Mexico." In Sylvia A. Hewlett and Richard S. Weinert, eds., *Brazil and Mexico: Patterns in Late Development*, pp. 57–109. Philadelphia, Pa.: Institute for the Study of Human Issues, 1982.

Conniff, Michael L. "Introduction: Towards a Comparative Definition of Populism." In Michael L. Conniff, ed., *Latin American Populism in Comparative Perspective*, pp. 3–30. Albuquerque: University of New Mexico Press, 1982.

———. *Urban Politics in Brazil: The Rise of Populism, 1925–1945.* Pittsburgh, Pa.: University of Pittsburgh Press, 1981.

Cornelius, Wayne. *Politics and the Migrant Poor in Mexico City*. Stanford, Calif.: Stanford University Press, 1975.

Coutinho, Marcia. "Regularização de Loteamentos: O Começo de uma Experiência no Rio de Janeiro." In Paulo F. Cavallieri, ed., *Quatro Estudos*, pp. 39–54. Rio de Janeiro: IPLANRIO, 1986.

Damatta, Roberto. *Carnavais, Malandros e Heróis: Para uma Sociologia do Dilema Brasileiro*. Rio de Janeiro: Zahar, 1979.

Della Cava, Ralph. "A Igreja e a Abertura, 1974–1985." In Paulo J. Krischke and Scott Mainwaring, eds., *A Igreja nas Bases em Tempo de Transição*, pp. 13–45. Pôrto Alegre, Brazil: CEDEC, 1986.

Dietz, Henry. *Poverty and Problem-Solving under Military Rule*. Austin: University of Texas Press, 1980.

Diniz, Eli. "A Transição Política no Brasil: Uma Avaliação da Dinâmica da Abertura." *Dados* 28(3) (1985): 329–346.

———. "Voto e Realinhamento Eleitoral no Rio de Janeiro." *C and P* 2(1–2) (1984): 77–99.

———. "Favela: Associativismo e Participação Social." In Renato R. Boschi, ed., *Movimentos Coletivos no Brasil Urbano*, pp. 27–74. Rio de Janeiro: Zahar, 1982.

———. *Voto e Máquina Política: Clientelismo e Patronagem no Rio de Janeiro*. Rio de Janeiro: Paz e Terra, 1982.

———. "Máquinas Políticas e Oposição: O MDB no Rio de Janeiro." *Dados* 23(3) (1980): 335–357.

———. *Empresário, Estado e Capitalismo no Brasil: 1930–1945*. Rio de Janeiro: Paz e Terra, 1978.

Diniz, Eli, Renato R. Boschi, and Renato Lessa, eds. *Modernização e Consolidação Democrática no Brasil: Dilemas da Nova República*. Rio de Janeiro: Edições Vértice and IUPERJ, 1989.

Downs, Charles. *Revolution at the Grassroots: Community Organizations in the Portuguese Revolution*. Albany: State University of New York, 1989.

Duncan Baretta, Silvio R., and John Markoff. "Brazil's Abertura: From What to What?" In James M. Malloy and Mitchell A. Seligson, eds., *Authoritarians and Democrats*, pp. 43–65. Pittsburgh, Pa.: University of Pittsburgh Press, 1987.

Durham, Eunice. "Movimentos Sociais: A Construção da Cidadania." *Novos Estudos* 10 (1984): 24–30.

Eckstein, Susan. *The Poverty of Revolution: The State and the Urban Poor in Mexico*. Princeton, N.J.: Princeton University Press, 1977.

———., ed. *Power and Popular Protest: Latin American Social Movements*. Berkeley: University of California Press, 1989.

Erickson, Kenneth P. *The Brazilian Corporative State and Working-Class Politics*. Berkeley: University of California Press, 1977.

Escobar, Arturo, and Sonia E. Alvarez, eds., *The Making of Social Movements in Latin America.* Boulder, Colo.: Westview Press, 1992.

Evans, Peter. *Dependent Development.* Princeton, N.J.: Princeton University Press, 1979.

Evans, Peter, Dietrich Reuschemeyer, and Theda Skocpol, eds. *Bringing the State Back In.* Cambridge: Cambridge University Press, 1985.

Evers, Tilman. "Identity: The Hidden Side of New Social Movements in Latin America." In David Slater, ed., *New Social Movements and the State in Latin America*, pp. 43–71. Amsterdam: CEDLA, 1985.

Fanon, Frantz. *The Wretched of the Earth.* London: MacGibbon and Kee, 1965.

Flynn, Peter. "Class, Clientelism and Coercion: Some Mechanisms of Internal Dependency Control." *Journal of Commonwealth and Comparative Politics* 12(2) (1974): 138–156.

Foweraker, Joe. *Making Democracy in Spain: Grass-roots Struggle in the South, 1955–1975.* Cambridge: Cambridge University Press, 1989.

Foweraker, Joe, and Ann L. Craig, eds. *Popular Movements and Political Change in Mexico.* Boulder, Colo.: Lynne Reinner, 1990.

French, John D. *The Brazilian Workers' ABC: Class Conflict and Alliances in Modern São Paulo.* Chapel Hill: University of North Carolina Press, 1992.

Gilbert, Alan, and Joseph Gugler, eds. *Cities, Poverty and Development: Urbanization in the Third World.* London: Oxford University Press, 1982.

Gilbert, Alan, and Peter Ward. *Housing, the State and the Poor.* Cambridge: Cambridge University Press, 1985.

Gohn, Maria da Glória. *Reivindicações Populares Urbanas: Um Estudo Sobre as Sociedades de Amigos de Bairro de São Paulo.* São Paulo: Edições Cortes, 1981.

Graham, Carol. "The APRA Government and the Urban Poor: The PAIT Programme in Lima's Pueblos Jóvenes." *Journal of Latin American Studies* 23 (1991): 91–130.

Graham, Douglas H., and Sérgio Buarque de Hollanda Filho. *Migrações Internas no Brasil: 1872–1970.* São Paulo: IPE/USP, 1984.

Graham, Richard. *Patronage and Politics in Nineteenth-Century Brazil.* Stanford, Calif.: Stanford University Press, 1990.

Hagopian, Frances, and Scott Mainwaring. "Democracy in Brazil: Problems and Prospects." *World Policy Journal* 4(3) (1987): 485–514.

Hahner, June E. *Poverty and Politics: The Urban Poor in Brazil, 1870–1920.* Albuquerque: University of New Mexico Press, 1986.

Hamilton, Nora. *The Limits of State Autonomy: Post-Revolutionary Mexico.* Princeton, N.J.: Princeton University Press, 1982.

Hellman, Judith. "The Role of Ideology in Peasant Politics: Peasant Mobilization and Demobilization in the Laguna Region." *Journal of Interamerican Studies and World Affairs* 25(1) (1983): 3–29.

Huntington, Samuel, and Joan Nelson. *No Easy Choice: Political Participation in Developing Countries.* New Haven, Conn.: Yale University Press, 1976.

Ianni, Octávio. *A Formação do Estado Populista na América Latina.* Rio de Janeiro: Civilização Brasileira, 1975.

IPLANRIO. *Morar na Metrópole: Ensaios Sobre Habitação Popular no Rio de Janeiro.* Rio de Janeiro: IPLANRIO, 1988.

————. *Contribuição aos Dados de População das Favelas do Município do Rio de Janeiro.* Rio de Janeiro: IPLANRIO, 1984.

Jacobi, Pedro. "Movimentos Sociais: Teoria e Prática em Questão." In Ilse Scherer-Warren and Paulo J. Krischke, eds., *Uma Revolução no Cotidiano? Os Novos Movimentos Sociais na América Latina,* pp. 246–275. São Paulo: Brasiliense, 1987.

Jaquette, Jane, ed. *The Women's Movement in Latin America: Feminism and the Transition to Democracy.* Boston: Unwin Hyman, 1989.

Jelin, Elizabeth. *Women and Social Change in Latin America.* London: United Nations Research Institute for Social Development and Zed Books, 1990.

Katznelson, Ira, and Aristide Zolberg, eds. *Working-Class Formation: Nineteenth-Century Patterns in Western Europe and the United States.* Princeton, N.J.: Princeton University Press, 1986.

Kaufmann, Robert. "The Patron–Client Concept and Macro-Politics: Prospects and Problems." *Comparative Studies in Society and History* 16 (1974): 284–308.

Keck, Margaret. "The New Unionism in the Brazilian Transition." In Alfred Stepan, ed., *Democratizing Brazil,* pp. 252–296. New York: Oxford University Press, 1989.

————. "Democratization and Dissension: The Formation of the Workers' Party." *Politics and Society* 15(1) (1986–87): 67–95.

Kowarick, Lúcio. "The Pathways to Encounter: Reflections on the Social Struggle in São Paulo." In David Slater, ed., *New Social Movements and the State in Latin America,* pp. 73–94. Amsterdam: CEDLA, 1985.

Lamounier, Bolivar, and Raquel Meneguello. *Partidos Políticos e Consolidação Democrática, o Caso Brasileira.* São Paulo: Brasiliense, 1986.

Leal, Victor Nunes. *Coronelismo, Enxada e Voto: O Município e o Regime Representativo no Brasil.* São Paulo: Alfa-Ômega, 1975.

Leeds, Anthony, and Elizabeth Leeds. *A Sociologia do Brasil Urbano.* Rio de Janeiro: Zahar, 1978.

Leeds, Elizabeth. "The State's Use of Criminal Violence to Mask Structural Violence: Cocaine and Folk-Heroes in the Favelas of Rio de Janeiro." Paper presented at the New England Council for Latin American Studies meetings (NECLAS), Wellesley College, Wellesley, Mass., 1988.

Lemarchand, René, and Keith Legg. "Political Clientelism and Development: A Preliminary Analysis." *Comparative Politics* 4 (1972): 149–178.

Lojkine, Jean. *Le Marxisme, l'État et la Question Urbaine.* Paris: PUF, 1977.

Macedo, Carmen Cinira. *Tempo de Genesis: O Povo das Comunidades Eclesiais de Base.* São Paulo: Brasiliense, 1986.

Machado da Silva, Luiz Antônio. "A Política na Favela." *Cadernos Brasileiros* 9(41) (1967): 35–47.

Machado da Silva, Luiz Antônio, and Alícia Ziccardi. "Notas para uma Discussão Sobre Movimentos Sociais Urbanos." *Cadernos do Centro de Estudos Rurais e Urbanos* 13 (1979): 79–95.

MacRae, Edward. "Homosexual Identities in Transitional Brazilian Politics." In Arturo Escobar and Sonia E. Alvarez, eds., *The Making of Social Movements in Latin America*, pp. 185–203. Boulder, Colo.: Westview Press, 1992.

Mainwaring, Scott. "Grassroots Popular Movements and the Struggle for Democracy: Nova Iguaçu." In Alfred Stepan, ed., *Democratizing Brazil*, pp. 168–204. New York: Oxford University Press, 1989.

———. "Urban Popular Movements, Identity, and Democratization in Brazil." *Comparative Political Studies* 20(2) (1987): 131–159.

———. "The Transition to Democracy in Brazil." *Journal of Interamerican Studies and World Affairs* 28 (1986): 149–179.

Martins, Luciano. "The 'Liberalization' of Authoritarian Rule in Brazil." In Guillermo O'Donnell, Philippe Schmitter, and Laurence Whitehead, eds., *Transitions from Authoritarian Rule: Latin America*, pp. 72–94. Baltimore, Md.: Johns Hopkins University Press, 1986.

———. *Estado Capitalista e Burocracia no Brasil Pós-64*. Rio de Janeiro: Paz e Terra, 1985.

Medina, Carlos A. *A Favela e o Demagogo*. São Paulo: Impressa Livre, 1964.

Mericle, Kenneth S. "Corporatist Control of the Brazilian Working Class: Authoritarian Brazil Since 1964." In James M. Malloy, ed., *Authoritarianism and Corporatism in Latin America*, pp. 303–338. Pittsburgh, Pa.: University of Pittsburgh Press, 1977.

Moisés, José Álvaro, ed. *Cidade, Povo e Poder*. Rio de Janeiro: Paz e Terra, 1981.

———. *Contradições Urbanas e Movimentos Sociais*. Rio de Janeiro: Paz e Terra, 1977.

Moisés, José Álvaro, and J. A. Guilhon Albuquerque, eds. *Dilemas da Consolidação da Democracia*. São Paulo: Paz e Terra, 1989.

Moreira Alves, Maria Helena. *State and Opposition in Military Brazil*. Austin: University of Texas Press, 1985.

———. "Grassroots Organizations, Trade Unions and the Church: A Challenge to Controlled Abertura in Brazil." *Latin American Perspectives* 2(11) (1984): 73–102.

Mouzelis, Nicos. "On the Concept of Populism: Populist and Clientelist Modes of Incorporation in Semiperipheral Polities." *Politics and Society* 14(3) (1985): 329–348.

Needell, Jeffrey. *A Tropical Belle Epoque: Elite Culture and Society in Turn-of-the-Century Rio de Janeiro*. Cambridge: Cambridge University Press, 1987.

Nelson, Joan. *Access to Power: Politics and the Urban Poor in Developing Nations*. Princeton, N.J.: Princeton University Press, 1979.

Nordlinger, Eric. *On the Autonomy of the Democratic State.* Cambridge, Mass.: Harvard University Press, 1981.

Nunes, Guida. *Favela: Resistência pelo Direito de Viver.* Petrópolis, Brazil: Vozes, 1980.

———. *Rio: Metrópole de 300 Favelas.* Rio de Janeiro: Vozes, 1978.

O'Donnell, Guillermo, Philippe Schmitter, and Laurence Whitehead, eds. *Transitions from Authoritarian Rule: Prospects for Democracy.* Baltimore, Md.: Johns Hopkins University Press, 1986.

O'Gorman, Frances. *Base Communities in Brazil.* Rio de Janeiro: Francisco Alves, 1983.

Olson, Mancur. *The Logic of Collective Action.* Cambridge, Mass.: Harvard University Press, 1971.

Ortiz, Renato. *A Consciência Fragmentada.* Rio de Janeiro: Paz e Terra, 1980.

Pang, Eul-Soo. "Coronelismo in Northeast Brazil." In Robert Kern, ed., *The Caciques*, pp. 65–88. Albuquerque: University of New Mexico Press, 1973.

Parisse, Lucien. *Favelas do Rio de Janeiro: Evolução e Sentido.* Rio de Janeiro: Centro Nacional de Pesquisas Habitacionais, 1969.

Pechman, Tema. "A Política de Intervenção em Áreas Faveladas: O Município do Rio de Janeiro." Paper presented at the Associação Nacional de Pós-Graduação e Pesquisa em Ciências Sociais meetings (ANPOCS), Friburgo, Brazil, 1982.

Perlman, Janice. *The Myth of Marginality: Urban Poverty and Politics in Rio de Janeiro.* Berkeley: University of California Press, 1976.

Petras, James. "State Terror and Social Movements in Latin America." *International Journal of Politics, Culture and Society* 3(2) (1989): 179–212.

Pires do Rio Caldeira, Teresa. *A Política dos Outros.* São Paulo: Brasiliense, 1984.

Ray, Talton. *The Politics of the Barrios of Venezuela.* Berkeley: University of California Press, 1969.

Rezende, Fernando. "O Crescimento (Descontrolado) da Intervenção Governamental na Economia Brasileira." In Olavo Brasil de Lima, Jr., and Sérgio H. Abranches, eds., *As Origens da Crise: Estado Autoritário e Planejamento no Brasil*, pp. 214–252. São Paulo: Edições Vértice, 1987.

Rio de Janeiro. "Á Margem, Cresce a Grande Cidade: Favela." *Revista do Tribunal de Contas do Município do Rio de Janeiro* 1 (1981): 53–60.

Rocha, Oswaldo P. "A Era das Demolições: Cidade do Rio de Janeiro: 1870–1920." Master's thesis, Instituto de Ciências Humanas e Filosofia, Níteroi, Brazil, 1982.

Roniger, Luis. *Hierarchy and Trust in Mexico and Brazil.* New York: Praeger, 1990.

Rothstein, Frances. "The Class Basis of Patron–Client Relations." *Latin American Perspectives* 6(2) (1979): 25–35.

Rush, Barbara. "From Favela to Conjunto: The Experience of Squatters Removed to Low-Cost Housing in Rio de Janeiro, Brazil." Honors thesis, Harvard College, Cambridge, Mass., 1974.

Saiz, Juan M. R. "Urban Struggles and Their Consequences." In Joe Foweraker and Ann L. Craig, eds., *Popular Movements and Political Change in Mexico*, pp. 234–246. Boulder, Colo.: Lynne Reinner, 1990.

Santos, Carlos N. F. "Metrópoles e Outras Cidades Brasileiras-Bem Antes de 60, Muito Depois de 80." *Espaço e Debates* 13 (1984): 103–116.

———. "Some Considerations About the Possibilities of Squatter Settlements Redevelopment Plans: The Case of Brás de Pina." Master's thesis, MIT, Cambridge, Mass., 1971.

Sarles, Margaret J. "Maintaining Political Control Through Parties: The Brazilian Strategy." *Comparative Politics* 15 (1982): 41–72.

Scherer-Warren, Ilse. "O Carater dos Novos Movimentos Sociais." In Ilse Scherer-Warren and Paulo J. Krischke, eds., *Uma Revolução no Cotidiano? Os Novos Movimentos Sociais na América Latina*, pp. 35–53. São Paulo: Brasiliense, 1987.

Schmitter, Philippe. *Interest Conflict and Political Change in Brazil*. Stanford, Calif.: Stanford University Press, 1971.

Schneider, Cathy. "Mobilization at the Grassroots: Shantytowns and Resistance in Authoritarian Chile." *Latin American Perspectives* 18(68) (1991): 92–112.

Scott, James C. *Weapons of the Weak*. New Haven, Conn.: Yale University Press, 1985.

———. "The Erosion of Patron–Client Relations and Social Change in Southeast Asia." *Journal of Asian Studies* 32(1) (1972): 5–37.

SECPLAN. *Bairros Populares e favelas*. Rio de Janeiro: SECPLAN, 1985.

Skocpol, Theda. *States and Social Revolutions: A Comparative Analysis of France, Russia and China*. Cambridge: Cambridge University Press, 1979.

Slater, David, ed. *New Social Movements and the State in Latin America*. Amsterdam: CEDLA, 1985.

SMDS. *Cadastro de Favelas*, vol. 3. Rio de Janeiro: Prefeitura da Cidade do Rio de Janeiro, 1983.

Solis, Sidney S. F., and Marcus V. T. Ribeiro. "O Rio Onde o Sol não Brilha: Acumulação e Pobreza na Transição para o Capitalismo." *Rio de Janeiro* 1 (1986): 45–59.

Stepan, Alfred. "State Power and the Strength of Civil Society in the Southern Cone of Latin America." In Peter Evans, Dietrich Rueschemeyer, and Theda Skocpol, eds., *Bringing the State Back In*, pp. 317–343. Cambridge: Cambridge University Press, 1985.

———. *The State and Society: Peru in Comparative Perspective*. Princeton, N.J.: Princeton University Press, 1978.

Stokes, Susan. "Politics and Latin America's Urban Poor: Reflections from a Lima Shantytown." *Latin American Research Review* 26(2) (1991): 75–101.

Tavares de Almeida, Maria Hermínia. "Novo Sindicalismo and Politics in Brazil." In John D. Wirth, Edson O. Nunes, and Thomas E. Bogenschild, eds., *State and Society in Brazil: Continuity and Change*, pp. 147–177. Boulder, Colo.: Westview Press, 1987.

Tilly, Charles, ed. *The Formation of National States in Western Europe*. Princeton, N.J.: Princeton University Press, 1975.

Trimberger, Ellen K. *Revolution from Above: Military Bureaucrats and Development in Japan, Turkey, Egypt and Peru*. New Brunswick, N.J.: Transaction Books, 1978.

Valenzuela, J. Samuel. "Labor Movements in Transitions to Democracy." *Comparative Politics* 21 (1989): 445–472.

Valla, Victor V. *Educação e Favela: Política para as Favelas do Rio de Janeiro*. Rio de Janeiro: Zahar, 1986.

———. *A Penetração Norte-Americano na Economia Brasileira, 1898–1928*. Rio de Janeiro: Livro Técnico S/A, 1979.

Valladares, Lícia do Prado. *Passa-Se uma Casa: Análise do Programa de Remoção de Favelas do Rio de Janeiro*. Rio de Janeiro: Zahar, 1978.

Vianna, Oliveira. *Instituições Políticas Brasileiras*. Rio de Janeiro: Distribuidora Record, 1974.

Vilaça, Marcos V., and Roberto C. de Albuquerque. *Coronel, Coroneis*. Rio de Janeiro: Tempo Brasileiro, 1965.

Vilas, Carlos. "El Sujeto Social de la Insurrección Popular: La Revolución Sandinista." *Latin American Research Review* 20(1) (1985): 119–147.

Weffort, Francisco. *O Populismo na Política Brasileira*. São Paulo: Paz e Terra, 1980.

Zaluar, Alba. *A Máquina e a Revolta*. São Paulo: Brasiliense, 1985.

Index